MARKS OF DISTINCTION

MARKS OF DISTINCTION

The Memoirs of Elaine Blond

WITH
BARRY TURNER

VALLENTINE, MITCHELL

First published 1988 in Great Britain by
VALLENTINE, MITCHELL & CO. LTD.
Gainsborough House, Gainsborough Road,
London, E11 1RS, England

and in the United States of America by
VALLENTINE, MITCHELL & CO. LTD.
c/o Biblio Distribution Centre
81 Adams Drive, P.O. Box 327, Totowa, N.J. 07511

British Library Cataloguing in Publication Data

Blond Elaine
    Marks of distinction : the memoirs of
    Elaine Blond.
    1. Great Britain. Philanthropy. Blond,
    Elaine
    I. Title   II Turner, Barry
    361.7'4'0924
    ISBN 0-85303-235-1

Library of Congress Cataloging-in-Publication Data

Blond, Elaine, d. 1985.
    Marks of distinction.

Includes index.
    1. Blond, Elaine, d. 1985.   2. Jews—England—
    Biography.   I. Turner, Barry.   II. Title.
    DS135.E6B583   1988   942'.004924024   88-26083
    ISBN 0-85303-235-1

Printed and bound in Great Britain by
A. Wheaton & Co. Ltd, Exeter

CONTENTS

ILLUSTRATIONS

Between pages 86 and 87

(All the photographs are taken from the author's collection.)

FOREWORD

An autobiography is inevitably the issue of many personal conflicts. In measures varying greatly from person to person, vanity contends with modesty, ambition with humility, prevarication with frankness. Illusion very often becomes reality in the mind of the writer. Elaine Blond's story of her life is not totally free of these conflicts, but her many friends will recognize the expression of her total integrity and her serious search for truth in the causes and events which filled that life so abundantly. Her triumph was to be loved and remembered by hundreds of ordinary people as well as many extraordinary ones. She lavished time, care and affection on airmen, doctors, teachers, social workers, artists, the disabled and the disadvantaged. She was passionately concerned with the young: orphans, refugees and aspiring students all absorbed her most vital efforts, and she maintained her interest in them individually throughout their careers. She was proud of their successes, she grieved for their failures, and she coaxed, bullied and encouraged each of them to give of his or her best. In turn they loved her, consulted her, argued with her and generally stimulated her to further acts of kindness and generosity.

Her modernity and freshness of thought were in sharp contrast to her sense of grandness and her propensity to Edwardian standards and values. She was eager to embrace new ideas, new technology and new fashion and design. Her leadership of the birth-control movement in Manchester in the 1920s, and the art nouveau collection in her house in Melbury Road in the 1930s, reflected her receptiveness to modernity, as did her key role in the experimental theatre of the Royal Court in the 1950s and 1960s.

Above all, she loved and responded to the cut and thrust of polemic. Whilst it was mainly with those closest to her that discussion sometimes became heated argument, she was fearless and outspoken in her views even with the grandest of contestants. She was at her best with her second husband Neville, the love of her life, who never ceased to exasperate and to stimulate her. Neville Blond combined an hilarious sense of humour with an unerring eye for weakness, both in ideas and individuals, and even at the height of their most furious arguments could make her dissolve into helpless laughter with a particularly well-timed and barbed aside. His was a more worldly character than Elaine's and he greatly widened her circle of interests and friends. Perhaps the most exciting venture for both of them arose from his appointment by Harold Wilson (then President of the Board of Trade) as what came to be described as British Trade Ambassador to the United States. Americans, who dubbed Neville Britain's Top Salesman, took to them both with warmth and admiration. The friendships which they formed at that time lasted until Elaine's death and she felt as much at home in New York as in London.

Elaine was the youngest of a remarkable Lancashire family, the children of Michael and Hannah Marks, Jewish immigrants from Russian Poland. She grew up at a time when her brother and sisters had reached great heights of achievement and recognition. She spent her life carving out her own niche and keeping as far as possible out of the shadow of the immense personal attainments of her siblings. In most of the issues about which they cared, the sisters were ferociously competitive (none except Rebecca had the temerity to compete with Simon).

Happily their chosen arenas centred on good works and good taste. Research Institutes and Fellowships, gardens, crèches, classrooms and hospital wards all over Britain and Israel bear the names of individual members of the family, as do scores of bursaries and scholarships.

The competition was a sweet one: each splendid project by one spurred the others on to yet greater effort and generosity. When Elaine helped rebuild the roof of the little church at Ashurst Wood, Miriam became the prime benefactor of her local church at Overton. Miriam acquired Berrydown, an elegant Lutyens house in Overton, and filled it with fine furniture and paintings selected with great discrimination over many years. Tilly thereupon bought Barton St Mary's, a Lutyens house in East Grinstead, and spent much time and love in decorating it with fine works of art and an exquisite collection of French Empire furniture. Elaine's country home, Gotwick Manor, near East Grinstead, was equally beautiful and the annual open day in her gardens was the admiration of the district and the envy of her sisters. The competition extended to clothing and jewellery. The sisters were regular and privileged clients of Worth, Hartnell, Dior and Schiaparelli as well as Boucheron, Asprey and Van Cleef and Arpels. It was grudgingly conceded that Tilly's collection of jewellery was ahead of her sister's, whilst Elaine's acute dress sense was matched only by that of her sister-in-law, Miriam Marks.

Of the four sisters, Rebecca and Elaine, the oldest and the youngest, were most alike. They were passionate and ambitious, they dreamed great dreams and achieved many of them. Both at the end felt they had left much undone. Where Miriam and Tilly were gentle and, in the main, fulfilled, Rebecca and Elaine were fierce and filled with the divine discontent of high aspiration.

Elaine's was a complex character, demanding of her friends and family, but more so of herself. Her diary, until the very day she died, was filled to the margins with meetings and appointments during the day, and drinks and dinners in the evening. Most of her activities centred upon good works – she spent little time purely on herself. Her weekends, however, were reserved for the country, at her beloved Gotwick, where she sought the company of those near and dear to her. Even here, as chairman of the Blond-McIndoe Trust, she was often frenetically occupied with meetings and discussions, and entertaining and accommodating her fellow trustees. The activities of the Research Unit and the milieu of the Queen Victoria Hospital provided Elaine not only with a great sense of achievement, but with a coterie of very special and close friends who understood her foibles, loved and admired her for her integrity and strength of purpose, and enriched her life immeasurably.

She believed passionately in Judaism as a creative and enobling set of values. Whilst she had little patience with orthodoxy of any nature, she did attend synagogue once a year, on the Day of Atonement, and she enjoyed Jewish traditional events such as the Passover Seder at Michael House. This great family reunion started by Israel Sieff in the 1950s continues today under the patronage of Marcus Sieff. Even the remotest members of the family, wives and ex-wives, husbands and ex-husbands, Jews and Christians alike, attend the ceremony, and Elaine loved the banter and the inevitable tensions as much as the event itself.

Not surprisingly, she believed strongly in the need for women to stand on their own and to be recognized for their individual talents. She was not, however, a passionate feminist like Rebecca, and she deferred to her brother Simon, as head of the family, throughout his lifetime. When her nephew Marcus assumed that mantle, Elaine unreservedly transferred her loyalty to him and continued, as ever, to afford him affection and respect, which he returned in good measure.

She took a great personal pride in the progress and reputation of the family business, Marks and Spencer. She was a regular shopper at the Marble Arch branch and she sent a flow of comment on the appearance or the quality of the goods to successive chairmen over many years. Her good taste in clothes and food was recognized by all the senior management of the business and her constructive criticism was greatly valued. She was inordinately proud when Marcus, whilst chairman, gave a luncheon for her at Michael House to present her with a gold watch in recognition of her contribution to the business.

Alongside of the Research Unit at East Grinstead, her most compelling interest lay in the State of Israel, her leading role in WIZO, and the Federation of Women Zionists of Great Britain. She led by example, tirelessly working to the last day of her life to harness both human and financial resources to the exclusive good of the women and children who are WIZO's beneficiaries. Throughout the sometimes acrimonious differences that arose in various committees through conflicts of personality or ambition, Elaine remained calm and full of sound, North Country common sense. Always a good listener, she was patient and sympathetic with the problems of 'her girls', and creative in the solutions and compromises she evolved. It was remarkable to see her transformation from an aloof and impatient grande dame to a gentle and understanding counsellor, when she felt it was appropriate. As a result, she was loved and respected as a friend as well as a leader.

Throughout a lifetime of creative and meaningful work Elaine used her wealth and her great talents with compassion and generosity, for the benefit of thousands of people in need, and with taste, so that her life was wholly admirable. Elaine Blond was indeed what the Bible describes as an 'Eshet Chayil' – a Woman of Value.

David Susman, 1988

Growing Up in Manchester

I remember Manchester as a quiet place. The illusion was created by an early upbringing on the plush north side of the city. There, at the turn of the century, large red-brick Victorian houses were segregated by spacious walled gardens and cobbled tree-lined roads. What traffic there was – mostly horse-drawn trade vehicles – moved at a sedate pace. If I was discouraged from playing in the street, it was more for social reasons than for worries about my safety. From about the age of five, I was allowed to go out to visit friends without the embarrassment of an adult escort, a first indication of an independent spirit, I like to think.

On these excursions, never more than a few hundred yards, I would occasionally see a convoy of heavy wagons bringing cloth from the Lancashire mills *en route* to the docks. A more frequent sight was an electric tram, still at that time something of a novelty. Just across the way from where my family lived at 396 Bury New Road, on the corner of Wellington Street, was a terminus where each evening business commuters were delivered back to their homes after a busy and doubtless noisy day in offices or factories close to the heart of Manchester. The building, originally stables for the horse buses, still stands with the legend Manchester Carriage Company clearly visible over the centre door. All other traces of the Broughton and Cheetham Hill tram run have long since disappeared as have most of the monuments to my childhood. Churches and pubs have survived the years quite well, I cannot help noticing, which may say something about the British sense of cultural priorities, but nearly all the old houses fell victim to the post-war fashion for high-rise reinforced concrete. My parents' house came down in the Blitz. The site is now occupied by a telephone exchange.

I was the first of the Marks family not to have to worry about money – the lack of it, at any rate. My father, Michael Marks, spent much of his life doing little else. He was brought up in a small town called Slonim, in eastern Poland, as a citizen of Imperial Russia. And so he might have remained had he not also been Jewish. As a teenager

1

he was caught up in the terrors of the pogroms. Like thousands of his compatriots who were made scapegoats for Russia's chronic economic and social ills, the best he could hope for was a future as an army conscript.

No doubt the irony of serving his persecutors by offering himself as cannon fodder was not lost on my father. He determined to escape, but where to? It was a familiar problem faced by up to two million Jews who were driven from Russian territories in this period. The main thrust of the exodus was towards the United States, the land of Liberty and Opportunity. The appeal of America was made yet more beguiling by the rags-to-riches stories transmitted over the grapevine. Even allowing for the appalling reality of the city ghettos experienced by most immigrants, a one-way ticket to New York was clearly favoured as the best chance to make good. So attractive was it that some of the more unscrupulous sailing masters were not above conning their passengers into paying for an Atlantic passage when their intention was never to venture beyond the North Sea. It is even possible that Michael was caught out in this way, since in my younger days there was talk in the family of his landing in Britain by mistake. Perhaps America was his intended destination.

My own guess is that he cut his suit to fit his cloth. Britain was the nearest country untarnished by violent anti-Semitism, the shortest and cheapest journey on offer. Also, it was natural to follow the example of his elder brother, Barnet, who had emigrated to Britain some years earlier. Fraternal assistance in helping a newcomer find his feet might reasonably have been expected. However, if this was the case, Michael was in for a disappointment. By the time he arrived, Barnet had already departed for the United States, where he joined the army of optimists hoping to make a fortune out of the Yukon gold rush. The experience evidently tamed his pioneering spirit because later he settled for running a store in Dawson City.

The year of decision for Michael was 1881 or 1882. In trying to determine his age at this time, we are left with an even wider margin of error. In the absence of a birth certificate, the best evidence is his naturalization papers which specify 1859 as his year of birth, or his marriage and death certificates which favour 1863. Possibly the habit of stripping away the years started as a ruse to avoid conscription into the Russian army. Alternatively, he may have believed that greater maturity would count in his favour when applying for British citizenship. All we can say for certain is that Michael was still a very young man when he set off to make his own way in the world.

Leaving Slonim must have caused some heartache, though family ties had been weakened by the early death of my grandmother. It is said that she died giving birth to Michael. Of my grandfather we know nothing. There was one brother, Ephraim, who was left behind. He came back into my father's life a few years later, when he too emigrated.

Of Slonim itself, there appears to have been little to inspire sentimental attachment. Contemporary accounts portray it as a run-down, no-hope sort of place, where the chief sources of employment were a distillery and several small breweries. Other businesses — tar, tiles and rope-making — were described as 'poorly developed' and housing was cramped and miserable. But Slonim could at least boast a market. In appearance it was not much to write home about — 'a dirty, scruffy ramshackle building with porch and tiled roof accommodating 150 small shops'. Still, it was a popular gathering point and may well have afforded Michael his first opportunity to observe that a living can be achieved even in the most unpromising circumstances.

Whatever the inspiration, by the time brother Ephraim dis-embarked in 1890 Michael was established as a respectable haberdasher serving the needs of working-class Leeds. True, his place of business was no more than a simple wooden stall in the covered market, but his flair for selling was already much in evidence. Above the trays of neatly arranged household items, from reels of cotton and lace handkerchiefs to soap candles and sealing wax, was emblazoned the legend: 'Don't ask the price, it's a penny'. The slogan may well have originated with the need to keep transactions simple. Michael was still hesitant in English and haggling over prices with Yorkshire housewives was undoubtedly beyond his linguistic powers. He soon realized, however, that the Penny Bazaar was an attraction in itself. It offered at once a wide choice of purchase, the freedom of unhurried selection and the chance of picking up a bargain. It was not long before the young entrepreneur was looking to extend his interests.

That he had got so far in such a short time was extraordinary. He had landed in this country with little more than the clothes he stood up in to adopt one of the few occupations open to a penniless immigrant. He became a pedlar, tramping the streets of Yorkshire towns and villages with his bag of wares thrown over his shoulder. It was a strenuous, all-weather job, not best suited to a man of slight build who never enjoyed good health.

His first lucky break was a chance meeting with Isaac Dewhurst, a wholesale merchant whose philanthropic nature disguised a shrewd business brain. The story goes that Michael borrowed his initial working capital of £5 from Dewhurst. This act of generosity paid off handsomely for both parties since dealings between the two companies have continued to the present day. Part of the Marks and Spencer centenary celebrations was the presentation to Dewhurst of a gold £5 coin.

Another stroke of fortune came in the shape of Hannah Cohen. Just twenty-one when she and Michael married in 1886, Hannah was intelligent, quick-witted and determined. Though like my father she was more at home speaking Yiddish, her grasp of English was excellent. She became a powerful support to my father's ambitions and a devoted parent.

Her first child died in infancy. Then came Simon in 1888, followed in quick succession by Rebecca, or Becky as she was best known, Miriam and Matilda (or Tilly). I was the late arrival, born ten years after my youngest sister.

While the family was growing up, Father was rarely to be seen. He was out and about constantly searching for new products. Success in Leeds led to the opening of Penny Bazaars in neighbouring towns – Castleford, Wakefield, Warrington and Birkenhead – and to the taking on of a partner.

Michael spent some time assessing the possibilities. He needed someone with an eye for administrative detail, an anchorman who could take care of the office routine while he devoted his energies to buying and selling. For the second time in his career a ticklish problem was solved with the help of Isaac Dewhurst. The wholesaler's chief cashier, Tom Spencer, was declared the ideal candidate. Marks and Spencer was formally registered in September 1894. Tom Spencer put in £300 for a fifty per cent share of the company.

By then my family had moved to Manchester, where they lived over the shop at 20 Cheetham Hill Road. 'Don't ask the price, it's

4

a penny' was painted in bold scarlet over the front of the store. The assurance of free admission, also proclaimed in large lettering, suggested the entertainment value of idle browsing which Michael was delighted to encourage. Today's browser was likely as not to be tomorrow's customer!

Cheetham Hill was then at the heart of a thriving Jewish community. Just across the street from the Marks house was the Great Synagogue, a sturdy edifice of Portland stone rivalling the Victorian splendour of such neighbouring buildings as the Town Hall and the Manchester Free Library. At the bottom of Cheetham Hill was an even more obviously Jewish district, but the crowded backstreets of Strangeways could by no stretch of the imagination be described as prosperous. The most attractive feature of the district around the prison was its liveliness on Sundays. Free from outside competition the shops pulled in business from a wide area of the city while simultaneously earning strenuous disapproval from puritan worthies, who opposed any exceptions to Sunday observance.

The expansion of Marks and Spencer continued apace. A growing feeling of prosperity in the country gave a welcome boost to the Penny Bazaars, which had a strong attraction for working-class people with some money to spare. Michael made sure of customers' interest by ever more skilful purchasing of stock. His margin was narrow, but he made a satisfactory profit by accelerating the flow of sales. It was a hard way to make a living, one which conventional businessmen were inclined to reject as too much effort for too little reward.

By 1900 there were twenty-four Penny Bazaars in market-halls and another twelve in shops. Their geographical spread now extended to Birmingham, Newcastle, Cardiff and London, where the first of a succession of Marks and Spencer stores was opened in 1899 in Southwark. Meanwhile, a new central office and warehouse was acquired in Manchester. It was a short way up Cheetham Hill in Derby Street, where my mother's brother, Jacob Cohen, had a warehouse. For ever in my childhood memories the solid red-brick building will be associated with the excitement of watching the skaters whirling about the ice-rink next door.

Success occasioned another family move, this time to Bury New Road. The latest house was only a mile or so from the shop on Cheetham Hill, but it was like a different world. Built in a heavy Victorian style which signalled means and respectability, Knoll House (it even had a name!) boasted eight bedrooms, accommodation for a live-in cook and maid, a big garden with a summer house and a handsome drive. We also had a telephone which seldom rang.

But if the Marks now resided in some splendour, their style of living remained distinctly modest. Knoll House was often the setting for family gatherings or sober business meetings but never for lavish entertainment. The furnishings, mostly dark and solid, were more utilitarian than decorative. My father never owned a car: he either walked to his office or travelled by public transport. It was almost as if he were reluctant to tempt fate by flaunting his wealth. As I think of it, however, it is more likely that he was too preoccupied with his work, which gave him enormous satisfaction, to bother about spending money. Knoll House was the declaration of commercial achievement, the highly visible proof that Michael Marks was to be taken seriously. Everything else, if not purely functional, was mere frivolity and not to be indulged in by a dedicated entrepreneur.

A little more than a year after the family was installed in Bury New Road, I was born on 14 April 1902. In addition to the usual gathering at such occasions, my arrival was witnessed by a young friend of Simon's called Israel Sieff. He was chasing about the house looking for Simon, who had promised to go with him to the zoo: 'I dashed into one room and there was a strange sight. Mrs Marks was in bed. A nurse was in the act of smacking a small pink object which she held in the hand. There was a yell. I gave a yell too – of mingled fright and embarrassment – and fled.' It was not, I must add, the only time that Israel fled at the sound of one of my yells, but subsequently I was able to dispatch him and other troublesome boys with slightly more dignity.

As the baby of the family I was not spoilt for contacts with my brother and sisters. They were already of an age when their interests had extended far beyond the nursery. As for Mother, while she was always gentle and considerate, I do not think she relished the prospect of reliving the experiences of early maternity.

I was closest to Miriam who, alone of the family, seemed positively to enjoy the company of an infant. My reputation as a rather beautiful child rested largely with her as she made me attractive dresses and bonnets to set off my long curly hair. Her reward was to accompany me on walks and to hear passers-by comment on her sewing and embroidery skills.

If Miriam's generous nature helped to give me reassurance and security, Simon's stern assumption of male hegemony worked in the opposite direction. He was fourteen when I was born and from the first moment we made contact until my teenage years I was in total awe of him. Miriam and Tilly always deferred to his wishes, and my parents idolized their son. Only Becky, by far the strongest-willed of all the sisters, was a match for Simon. Later when I got to understand him a little better, I realized that he was probably as uncomprehending of me as a child as I was of him as an assertive and self-confident teenager. Certainly he did his best to ignore my existence. Israel Sieff once told me how on a rare occasion when Simon was left in charge of the infant, I was put tummy down across his lap as a support for his newspaper.

My happiest early memory of Simon was his extended visit to Nuremberg – not for his absence, but for his triumphal return when he presented me with a most wonderful collection of toys. It must be said that his generosity was not entirely selfless. Nuremberg was the centre of a thriving German toy industry and it was to find new products, as well as to learn the language, that Simon had been despatched there. No doubt, I was part of his market research; the ultimate assurance of the appeal and durability of items that were soon to appear on the display counters of the Penny Bazaars. It is incredible now to think of the range and sophistication of the toys that came within the Marks and Spencer pricing policy. I had great fun with a miniature sewing-machine complete with moving treadle, a paddle-steamer and a clown who beat a drum, as well as tops, rattles and squeakers, all of which were actually called Penny Toys.

My expectations of Simon's next foreign excursion – to Paris – were naturally high. In the event I had to make do with some rolls of material, which Miriam duly transformed into pretty dresses. If I seemed ungrateful, as no doubt I was, it was commendable of my sisters to resist pointing out that I was the only Marks daughter not to have to rely on hand-me-downs.

At the time, Simon's apparent need to travel was a mystery to me though I soon came to realize that it was an essential part of his business education. He had Father to thank. Michael was a true European in the sense that he was quick to see the possibilities of dealing directly with manufacturers across the Channel. In this way he cut out the middleman – and an unnecessary percentage – while extending his choice of product. The annual pilgrimage to the Leipzig trade fair was probably the single most important date in his calendar.

None of this may sound too surprising in the modern context, but we are talking of the days when English manufacturers were reluctant even to acknowledge their continental rivals. It came as a genuine surprise to some of them that Michael was prepared to challenge their claim to easy superiority. But the shock was greater for the competitors of the 'original' Penny Bazaar, who could not hope to match the sheer variety of goods supplied by Marks and Spencer.

Having taken naturally to the business, Simon was enthralled by the prospects of scaling yet greater heights. Still barely at an age of understanding, I was more concerned about my next meal and the chances of being allowed out to play.

My closest friend shared with me the problem of accommodating an older family. Teddy Sieff was the youngest of five children of whom the senior was Israel. Their father was a successful cloth merchant, who had moved into Bury New Road shortly before our arrival. As my mother was fond of reminding me, their house was not as grand as ours – it was smaller and part of a terrace – but it was a warm and friendly place, an irresistible attraction to me when life at Knoll House was weighed down by business conversation. I particularly enjoyed having lunch with Teddy, a ritual which was always preceded by a scathing comment from Mother: 'What do you want to go there for? They only give you bones.' However, my request was never refused. After a rigorous smartening up, I set off on the short walk to my friend's house. On the way I had to pass the Greek Orthodox Church, a building of cathedral grandeur and proportions which overshadowed all the surrounding houses. It was respected by my parents as an impressive monument to an earlier generation of immigrant traders. For a child it was too large to be lovable.

Teddy had a wicked sense of humour, a quality which excited me but at the same time made me apprehensive. I knew I could not get away with the things he did, but I was never quite sure how far his luck extended. Consequently, I was usually the voice of reason urging him, not always successfully, against such japes as sticking a pin in the cleaning lady as she bent over her dusting. On the whole my influence must have been for the good, since it was I who was nominated to take charge when the two of us were enrolled at a small private school known as The Mount. It was a responsibility I was soon to regret.

Released from the family reins, however loosely tied, Teddy gave himself heart and soul to the pursuit of anarchy. Mrs Shore, a demure lady of advancing years, began well with warnings of retribution if Teddy did not mend his ways. But after a few days her resolution evaporated and, instead of punishment, Teddy found himself in receipt of numerous prizes – apparently in recognition of an agile brain, but more probably given in the hope that where threats had failed, bribery might prove more effective.

Meanwhile, my exemplary behaviour went entirely unnoticed, at least at school. In the Sieff household, I was treated much more as the star turn, particularly by Mrs Sieff who pressed on me the choicest confectionery, assuring me always it was 'the very best'. My mother was not impressed, 'What is this nonsense of very best?' she demanded to know. 'You can't do better than the best.'

Apart from my close association with the Sieffs, I cannot say that my early upbringing was particularly Jewish. At a time when Zionism had barely touched the imagination of British Jewry, the natural inclination of the leading business families was towards assimilation with the dominant culture. Certainly that was the fashion in our immediate neighbourhood, where Jewish families were a small minority.

Visits to the Higher Broughton Synagogue were rare and usually linked to High Holy Days like Yom Kippur and Passover. But we were friendly with Rabbi Lewandowski. His grandson, Jan, who was a near contemporary of mine, sensibly abbreviated his surname to Lewando before embarking on a highly successful business career, much of it with Marks and Spencer.

As a child my only contact with the rigours of orthodoxy was a somewhat formal acquaintance with my uncle Ephraim. He was a tall, broad-shouldered man, whose jutting beard emphasized his stern, humourless nature. I was fascinated by his right hand which was missing one finger. He had left it in the Crimea, where he had fought as a Russian conscript.

Anyone less like my father it is difficult to imagine, but the two brothers managed to get along. Ephraim's chosen area of business was Scotland where he set up a chain of bazaars, but he lived in Manchester and was for a short time a director of Marks and Spencer.

Ephraim's domestic routine was strictly in accord with Jewish convention. Heads were covered at every meal, milk and meat were kept apart whether on the table or in the kitchen, and ham was treated like poison. Even on the most informal occasions women were herded off as second-class citizens, while children were to be seen but most definitely not heard. The proudest moment for Ephraim came when he was elected first president of the United Synagogue, in its time a notable addition to the civic architecture of Cheetham Hill. I often wonder what he would say if he could see it now – as a Panorama Cash and Carry.

I was barely five when my father died. I do not remember being told the news. It was just that one day he was there and the next he was gone – and the next, and the next. I heard later that he had been taken ill in the street. After the first shock there was comfort in the doctor's assurance that recovery would follow a complete rest. And so it seemed, for a day or two. Then, one evening, my father's condition suddenly worsened and he fell into a coma. He died on the last day of 1907.

My memories of him – real memories not just those handed down to me by the family – are slight. I do have a clear recollection of his weekly visit to the Working Men's Club (a fair indication that he had not let success go to his head) because he always brought me home a stick of May Queen rock, a sweet and sticky substance which appealed to my infant palate. Also, I remember him introducing me to the manager of the Midland Bank, quite the most important person I had met up to then.

That is about it really. But if we go on to ask what lasting influence my father had on me, I can be more expansive. That he was an exceptional businessman, no one can doubt. He was also a man of courage and conviction. He never forgot what it was like to be poor and he did much to help others fight their way out of poverty. I am convinced that the Marks and Spencer reputation for staff care can be traced back to his founding principles. It was he who ordered wooden platforms to be put behind the market-stalls (a modest innovation by today's standards, but welcomed then by assistants who had trouble keeping their feet warm) and installed gas-rings for staff to heat their lunches.

To summon up a mental picture of my father on the spur of the moment is to see him in his younger days as a penniless refugee looking for a home. It is an image that is reinforced by my own involvement with another generation of refugees – the children who fled from Nazi Germany. Many of them have made good too, I am pleased to think.

With Father gone, the family lost its sense of direction, even for a time its sense of purpose. Mother withdrew into herself. It is not difficult to understand why. She and Michael had worked so hard to succeed against all the odds. Now, having reached a stage in her life when she felt entitled to relax a little, the prospect of enjoyment was snatched away. She survived for ten years, but the grey sadness never left her face.

From the day of Father's death, the full responsibility for the family and its fortune passed to Simon. He was nineteen, an age when the outward show of self-confidence can hide a multitude of fears. In the years ahead he needed every ounce of determination and if, frequently, his manner was over-assertive and arrogant, I cannot help thinking that it was as much an act to boost his own resolution as to put down his opponents.

The toughest challenge came first. Premature death – not only Father's, but also that of Tom Spencer who had drunk himself into an early grave – put at risk the control of the company the two men had founded. Like Simon, the young Spencer was not old enough to claim direct representation on the board of directors. Instead, their interests were assumed by two executors, one of whom, William Chapman, the Spencer nominee, blatantly pursued his campaign to win power on his own behalf.

With no backing from Tom Spencer Junior, nor indeed from the Marks family executor, Simon declared his intention to fight. His strategy was to buy shares whenever they came on the market – a costly affair because he was always in competition with Chapman. At the same time, he had to resist efforts by his rivals to increase the share capital since the family reserves, though substantial, were not equal to buying up a new issue. Chapman, on the other hand, was in a better position to raise money.

As business prospered, the struggle for control became yet more frantic. In 1913, two years after he managed to gain a place on the

11

board, Simon was offering three times the going rate for shares held outside the family. Gradually, he built up his strength to a point where he could influence the composition of the board. One of the new directors he managed to appoint was his closest friend, Israel Sieff.

The climax of the takeover saga came in 1916, when Simon resorted to the law to frustrate Chapman's efforts to limit membership of the board to his own nominees. Simon's victory, confirmed on appeal, led to Chapman's resignation. In August 1916 Simon took over as chairman of the company. He was twenty-nine.

Though not entirely beyond my understanding, the drama of high finance that absorbed the rest of the family was for me incidental. The problems of a pubescent schoolgirl were quite enough to keep my brain occupied.

In the early spring of 1912 I was registered at the Manchester High School for Girls, where a place was found for me in the middle grade of the second form. Apart from being the only girls' school in the city thought suitable for the daughters of the prosperous middle class, Manchester High had a special attraction for Jewish parents because it was non-denominational. Thus an attempt to satisfy all factions of Christianity turned out to be of enormous benefit to the non-Christian community. The concession was not intended, but was accepted gratefully none the less.

I was not, at first, attracted to formal education. Much was expected of me and I was not at all sure that I could deliver. The tone was set in a brief first-day interview with the headmistress, the redoubtable Miss Sarah Burstall. She was glowing in her praise of Miriam and Becky, who had preceded me at the school. 'You're following in the path of two brilliant sisters,' she told me. 'I am sure you will live up to their example.' The word that came out was 'Yes'. The word I wanted to come out was 'Maybe'.

Manchester High was one of the spate of girls' public schools which came to prominence in the last quarter of the nineteenth century. Born of the conviction shared by an enlightened minority of business and professional people that the female intellect might respond to a little care and attention, the girls' schools followed the tradition of their male counterparts while trying not to lose sight of what were regarded as essentially feminine virtues. This led to some odd compromises as demonstrated by the Mistress of Girton

College, who urged her sports enthusiasts: 'If you must play hockey, try to hit the ball gently.'

Sarah Burstall was of like mind, but expressed herself more forthrightly. 'Games overexcite girls,' she told parents, 'and take too much out of them.' On matters of intellect, however, she made no concessions to claims of male dominance. Of sharp mind and even sharper temper if she felt thwarted, she made her great aim in life the broadening of the curriculum to suit girls of all abilities and aspirations. On the academic side this meant a growing emphasis on science, hitherto neglected by most girls' schools, with botany as a lead subject. In 1918, the year before I left school, there were no less than twenty-five old girls studying medicine at Manchester University. But there was also plenty of scope for practical subjects. There are times even now when I wish I had taken advantage of the much praised courses in domestic science. Somehow, the ability to turn out the simplest dish always escaped me. Then, as now, the mere sight of a kitchen filled me with dread.

It took a little while to get to know Miss Burstall. When I first arrived at the school, she was at the peak of her career, a tightly laced woman of middling years whose force of character was suggested by a firm gaze and a determined smile, which stopped well short of open laughter. She spoke to me often, mainly I think, in deference to the memory of my sisters, but once I broke the barrier of monosyllabic responses I found her warm and sympathetic.

Before I could concentrate on settling in at the school, I had to get used to the experience of long-distance travel – right the way across Manchester with a midway change of tram. A recent letter from a friend of those days reminds me of the pioneering spirit which inspired our arduous journey. Few of us had ever before ventured to the heart of Manchester. My experience was limited to a fleeting view of brightly lit shops from the back seat of a car. But once the crowded streets, the smell of horses and petrol fumes became routine, I began to discover the compensation of living in a big city. It was but ten minutes' walk from Dover Street, where our Gothic edifice of learning dominated the scene, to the centre of town. There I discovered a vegetarian restaurant that was well suited to accommodate the traditional Jewish diet. More to the point, its standard of catering was far superior to the school kitchens, where appetites were deadened by runny greens and soggy puddings.

My argument for going out to lunch, couched in suitably pious terms, swayed Miss Burstall but failed to take in the other girls, who were madly jealous of my hard-won privilege. Later, however, other Jewish girls caught on to the idea, until there was quite a party of us deserting the school at midday.

There were strict rules as to the route we were to follow. Oxford Road, a wide and busy thoroughfare, was considered safe for unaccompanied girls, but Portsmouth Street, though entirely respectable with its clean terraced houses and privet-lined gardens, was thought to be too quiet to be secure. This did not stop us from venturing into Portsmouth Street, which cut out a lot of unnecessary walking, but our courage stopped short at Grafton Street, also out of bounds, where from a distance we could see bare-footed children playing in the gutters.

My other victory over convention was in the choice of headgear. By way of uniform, the school favoured the customary gym slip crowned by a stiff boater with a wide brim. It was ungainly, uncomfortable and unfashionable. It also gave me headaches, or so I chose to believe. Miss Burstall was understanding. I converted to a panama on which I bestowed a semblance of individuality by attaching a yellow ribbon.

Academically, I got off to a reasonable start by gaining a junior school scholarship. In truth the intellectual exertion was more than strenuous, requiring as it did a feel for patriotism more than a solid academic grounding. 'What has Manchester done to help in this Great War?' my examiners demanded to know. I then had to write informative paragraphs about Kitchener's army, a submarine, a Zeppelin and a Dreadnought. Even the mathematics questions were given a chauvinistic edge. One conundrum required to know the expense in running a Red Cross hospital for eighteen months, assuming seventy beds each incurring a ten-shilling maintenance charge and other sundry expenses. I underestimated badly, not for the last time, in assessing the cost of charitable enterprises.

In fact, I quite enjoyed maths, which is more than I can say for singing lessons, presided over by the only male teacher in the school, and gymnastics. In both subjects I was encouraged to keep a low profile – silent in one, immobile in the other. But while an inability to hit the high notes or any other notes for that matter was no great deprivation, I did regret my athletic shortcomings. In an

14

environment where the display of female attractions was actively discouraged, Miss Bourne, the gym mistress, was alone in having the right to show off her legs. She did so to excellent effect.

At the head of a class of gawky young ladies, she led our physical jerks with a grace and style that belied the woodenness of Swedish drill. 'POSITION! HIPS – FIRM! POSITION! repeat – ONE TWO! rePOSE. POSITION! feet CLOSE! feet OPEN! repeat – ONE TWO! rePOSE!' and so on. To emulate Miss Bourne, I reasoned, was to discover the secret of perfect womanhood. Sadly an inability to co-ordinate arm and leg movements denied me the chance to test my theory.

The Manchester High of my youth was a Spartan establishment though no longer positively unhygenic. Electricity had been installed, thus avoiding a repetition of the incident in which a His Majesty's Inspector, arriving on a foggy day, found the classroom windows closed and all the gas lamps at full blast. 'The atmosphere', he reported, 'can be more easily imagined than described.' We also had a new drainage system – not before time, it was hinted darkly. While applauding these practical amenities, the pupils would doubtless have welcomed a few home comforts. That we were not so indulged – the memory of hard seats and draughty corridors still rankles – was less to do with the lack of funds than with the firm desire of Miss Burstall and her staff to turn our thoughts to serious matters.

We were taught the virtue of sacrifice, the duty to serve – and not just our future husbands and children. There was the wider community to consider. Miss Burstall was an avid collector of good causes and public responsibilities, not all of which were approved by her employers. Her devotion to the women's movement, for instance, raised a few eyebrows especially when, in my second year, she took part in a protest demonstration from Manchester to Stockport, riding in the back of a lorry. The opposition, who were also out in force, pelted the suffragettes with small stones.

It was a matter of some pride to Miss Burstall, as to the rest of us who were converts to sexual equality, that the three Pankhurst daughters attended Manchester High. What we did not know then was that Miss Burstall's predecessor, the first headmistress, Miss Elizabeth Day, had done her best to prevent their admission on the grounds that their father was a republican and an atheist. The pace of social change was evidently quickening.

Even sex was no longer taboo. How could it be with botany as a major subject and medicine as a favoured occupation. Nothing frivolous was tolerated, of course, though one of our teachers, Mrs Helen Watson, managed to get her Mills and Boon romantic novels (*The Captain's Daughter* and *Love the Intruder*) recognized in the High School list of staff publications. As if for decency's sake, her titles were flanked on one side by a sound basic text, *Modern Touch-Typing*, and on the other by a respectable if little-known work, *Irish Influence in Early Icelandic Literature*.

Evidence that girls could develop minds of their own disturbed some parents, who feared a breakdown of family discipline. Within my own family, there was a wide division between Simon, who was a rigid conservative in such matters, and Becky, who believed that we girls were capable of moving mountains and had every intention of proving her point. I had Becky as much as Manchester High to thank for the wayward spirit that was beginning to take hold of me.

In one sense, however, it was Becky who managed to put a large stumbling-block in my way, though it was the last thing on earth that she intended. Having discovered Zionism and thrown herself wholeheartedly into the campaign to found a Jewish home in Palestine, Becky decided that I should set an example to the rest of the generation by learning Hebrew. I was aghast; the school no less so. Teachers of Hebrew were notable by their rarity and were certainly not part of the High School establishment. As a final irony, Simon weighed in on my side, but in vain. A tutor was found and my plea not to be different was overruled.

What became known as 'Elaine's extras' caused me much anguish and frustration, which I projected on to my unfortunate teacher. Poor Mr Lewandowski. A gentle intellectual plucked from the burgeoning ranks of our local rabbi's family, he was torn between the attraction of steady and, so it looked, long-term employment and the dreadful prospect of daily incarceration with a resentful schoolgirl. I did well enough with Hebrew to pass the school certificate, but when it came to university entrance, the problems of communicating in a minority language were starkly revealed. The examiners, who were evidently of the old school, declared that they could not understand my Hebrew script. I had to go back to translate all my answers into Hebrew print. The effort might have been worthwhile if success had depended exclusively on my linguistic ability. But in those days, Hebrew was not accepted as a university subject in its own right. Achievement in the more conventional academic sphere counted for all. Since my efforts here had suffered by neglect, I was left high and dry with a good working acquaintance of the first Jewish language without the necessary basis for giving it practical application. Sadly, no one hit on the obvious solution, which was to extend my knowledge of Hebrew to a second oriental language.

As the first Manchester High girl to study Hebrew, I must at least have started a trend. Today, I am told, a quarter of the sixth form is familiar with the language. I suppose I should not be surprised. Manchester High has scored some notable advances over the years. As early as 1962, when Becky, Miriam, Tilly and I funded a new library for the school, I was amazed to find that recent additions to the curriculum included atomic physics and nuclear energy. It all seemed a far cry from my youthful excursions into higher learning. There was a time, I reminded myself, when a clear recollection of the flags of all the nations took precedence over the mysteries of thermodynamics.

The feeling of isolation at school brought on by the peculiarities of my education was paralleled by life at home, where, again, I was the odd one out. Being so much younger than everyone else was no great hardship while there were plenty of people around and the house bustled with activity. But after a succession of courtships, the Marks presence in Bury New Road was sharply depleted. I was not abandoned exactly but so often, as I played alone in one of the large and over-furnished rooms, I fancied I might just as well have been.

Becky was the first to go. Brushing aside family reservations, she decided to marry the boy next door – Israel Sieff. There were objections too from Israel's parents. At twenty-one, he was far too young to know his own mind, they argued, echoing to the word Mother's feelings about Becky. But with two such stubborn characters, opposition was counter-productive as, soon, everyone came to recognize. The only thing to do was to make the best of it or, as Mrs Sieff might have said, the 'very best' of it.

A full Jewish wedding is a magnificent spectacle at any time, but Becky and Israel touched the heights; literally so, for they held their ceremony and reception on the roof of the Midland Hotel. Then the unrivalled setting for any grand social event in Manchester,

17

the Midland excelled itself. Long tables with crisp white cloths which crackled in the summer breeze were loaded with every sort of delectable fare. The guests, gourmets one and all, were in correspondingly jolly mood.

Simon was best man. Becky and we sisters were all in white. Mine was a frothy dress, which I showed off to good effect to everyone prepared to take notice of an eight year old. Of all the children there, Teddy Sieff ate most; he was also the only one who was sick.

There was another Marks–Sieff wedding five years later, in 1915, when Simon married Israel's sister Miriam. This time, Israel was best man. He presided over an event that was more subdued than his own nuptials. The first anniversary of the Great War was an obvious neutralizer to any celebration, but on a more domestic level this was also a critical time for Marks and Spencer where Simon was still fighting for the ascendancy.

Later that same year, it was the turn of my second oldest sister, Miriam, to choose a partner. Her decision came as something of a surprise. Harry Sacher, her prospective husband, was over fifteen years her senior. But he was also a leading figure in Manchester Jewry, a notable intellectual who wrote leaders for the *Manchester Guardian*. In many ways he was a difficult man, one who defied contradiction from any but his academic equals. Needless to say, I did not figure in this select group.

The most memorable aspect of Miriam's wedding was the honeymoon – the sheer scale of it. We saw them off on a world tour, an erratic journey which climaxed with a visit to Peking. Occasional postcards kept us marginally informed of their progress.

With Miriam's departure, there were just three of us at home: me, Mother and Tilly. So far in this story, Tilly has barely made an appearance, which might be thought curious as I saw more of her than of the rest of the family put together. Yet, while Tilly was ever present, she was not really a close part of my early life. From childhood to her middle years, Tilly suffered from epilepsy, an affliction which defied treatment until well into the century. Her fits, sometimes followed by blackouts, were unpredictable and, for those who were not close to her, unnerving. School was thought to be out of the question, so Tilly was educated privately by a governess who came to the house each day. Inevitably, there was a huge sadness in Tilly's life. She wanted desperately to be accepted, but with

Becky and Miriam streaking ahead, she lost contact with her own generation. Meanwhile, I was coming up fast on the outside track, a constant reminder to Tilly of what might have been. Never once did she show me any resentment but later, when I had acquired a more sensitive understanding, I realized how lonely she must have felt. A sort of happiness came to her eventually, but she had a long wait.

She was in her forties before she took charge of her own life. Then she made up for all the lost years by spending money as if it were going out of fashion. Tilly's destiny was to excel us all in lavish entertainment and outré festivities. By far the naughtiest of the Marks sisters, Tilly never aspired to the feminine ideal. But she liked the idea of marriage and when the opportunity came, at the age of fifty-five, she took it. Simon, who by then was at the height of his power, objected but, for once, was overruled by the rest of the family.

After Simon and Miriam left home, we few who remained moved to a much smaller house out further towards Kersal. It was a practical decision which I heartily opposed. Our new address, a semi-detached Victorian villa, was gloomy inside and out. No doubt something could have been made of it, but circumstances were against any genuine attempt at home-making. Mother was frail and spent a lot of time in her room. Tilly, likewise, kept much to herself. When, frequently, I returned from school in that lackadaisical mood assumed by most teenagers when faced with household chores, I felt compelled to ring Miriam to ask advice on what to eat for supper. But no doubt what I really wanted was not food but attention.

It was Miriam, ever the kindliest sister and by now a stylish and sophisticated lady (she promoted her image by the use of an exceedingly long cigarette holder), who provided the brightest moments by taking me out for evenings in Manchester. What excitement! Manchester then had many claims to superiority over London. It was a greater centre of industrial power, and though extremes of wealth and poverty were always in evidence, private fortunes could often bring a direct public benefit. With the zealous support of merchants and manufacturers, who doubtless felt the need for cultural uplift, the arts flourished. Manchester was the city of concert halls, galleries and theatres. Whether it was the Hallé Orchestra at the Free Trade Hall or ballet at the Princes or experimental theatre at the Hornimans, the audiences were always enthusiastic and appreciative. The first play I ever saw was at the Manchester Gaiety, something called *Kattawampus*, of which there is no memory except the title. I went straight from school and sat in the gallery.

My great love was the ballet. I saw Pavlova for the first time in Manchester. Thereafter I followed her career devotedly. I was at the Coliseum in London on the saddest of nights in 1931, when a few hours after Pavlova's death the orchestra played the Dying Swan while the spotlight followed her ghost across the empty stage.

The war in Europe was a marginal influence on my life. This was partly a matter of age. Young people can tolerate the most monstrous events if they do not impinge greatly on their daily routine. But it must also be said that within the Jewish community, the war did not inspire wild displays of chauvinism. To fight for Britain was one thing, but to sacrifice lives for Russia, Britain's ally, called for a superhuman act of reconciliation. For many Jews, Russia was the enemy and would remain so until memories of the early pogroms were swept away by a mightier wave of anti-Semitism.

None the less, in my small circle I soon got used to the sight of khaki uniforms. Thrilled by the older brothers of school-friends who seemed to spend their leave parading for our inspection, I was enormously impressed when Simon joined up. This was just a few weeks after he had been made chairman of Marks and Spencer, a responsibility he took with him into the army. The board followed his progress round various northern postings, holding meetings in local pubs and hotels at times convenient to the military.

But of all the young men who went to war, the most romantic and dashing figure in my eyes was a friend of Simon's, a contemporary at Manchester Grammar. Neville Blond startled us all by donning the uniform of the Royal Horse Guards, a regiment tied to a narrow social brand of officer recruitment which most emphatically did not encompass many first- or second-generation immigrant families. Neville was from the middle ranks of Manchester business (his father was a jeweller), but it was not money so much as a sense of style that was his passport to achievement.

He was good-humoured, open-minded and urbane – the party guest everyone wanted to meet. His grasp of languages distinguished him as a staff officer in France, where he was one of the few able to communicate directly with our leading allies. A major by the age of twenty-two, he was twice mentioned in dispatches and was awarded the *Croix de Guerre* and the *Légion d'honneur*. He was very handsome in his uniform. My feelings for him were the closest I had come to falling in love.

Neville had what used to be called 'a good war'. The antithesis was Israel Sieff's youngest brother William, a gentle and withdrawn teenager whose single act of bravado was to join the army against the express wishes of his parents. The insensitivity of a military bureaucracy, which judged all men as fit to fight, was compounded by the treatment meted out to William in his first weeks of training. When letters stopped coming through, Israel went down to his camp at Aldershot to find out what was wrong. The boy was in solitary confinement – a bare cell without light or proper ventilation. He had been there for ten days after committing a minor but unspecified offence against army convention. Israel got him into hospital, but not soon enough to forestall a total mental and physical breakdown. He never recovered, though he lived on in a nursing-home, a cruel reminder of inhumanity on the home front. My single recollection of William is of a boy sitting quietly in a corner twisting a curl of hair on his finger. It is painful to realize that he did little else for the next fifty years.

For me, the war ended with a hastily summoned school assembly, an emotional declaration from Miss Burstall and a spirited rendering of 'God Save the King'. But by then my imagination was beset by other battles, which were only just beginning.

I was an early and willing convert to Zionism. Apart from my struggles with the complexities of Hebrew, which I was determined to put to some practical purpose, circumstances favoured an early grounding in the arguments for a Jewish national home in Palestine. From the early years of the century to midway through the war, Chaim Weizmann, the undisputed Zionist leader, made his home in Manchester. As a centre of Jewish influence, Manchester was unrivalled in Britain, but it was also the favoured home of Weizmann's fellow countrymen, the Russian Jews. Their awareness of anti-Semitism, often made more acute by first-hand experience, enhanced the attraction of Zionism.

Within the family, Weizmann was on close terms with Becky and Israel, Harry Sacher and Simon. As a frequent visitor to their homes, I saw quite a lot of the Weizmanns and listened, fascinated,

21

to reports of struggles within and beyond the Jewish community to win support for the Zionist ideal.

Weizmann was a slender figure with a thin face and bright, clear eyes. With his close-cut triangular beard, he preceded the image made world famous by Lenin. Like the Russian leader it was his gift for conveying a passionate self-confidence which defied contradiction. It was extraordinary that Weizmann's leadership was not underpinned by election or formal office. He did it all on sheer force of personality.

Israel and Becky were captivated from their first meeting with Weizmann, which took place just before the war at a friend's dinner party. Israel was by then already a committed Zionist. So too was Harry Sacher. He could date his conversion from the 1890s, when the Hungarian Theodor Herzl was devoting what was left of his short life to holding together a fragile alliance of European Jews who dreamed of a national home. It was Harry who forged the links between Weizmann and C.P.Scott, the legendary editor of the *Manchester Guardian* and a powerful, independent advocate of Zionism.

Simon was a late entrant. Preoccupied with business, he was less sure of himself in political matters. He might even have been a little jealous of Becky, who scorned his reserve but none the less deterred him from competing on ground where she was undoubtedly the master. It is not, I feel, entirely coincidental that Simon only came into his own when the centre of power moved beyond Becky's sphere of influence to London. With the setting up of the Palestine Bureau at 170 Piccadilly, Simon took charge of the administration.

That there were offices to occupy, or indeed any semblance of organization, was largely thanks to Israel. Having decided that Weizmann was the future of Zionism, he immediately put himself at the head of a fund-raising campaign. His success made him the natural second-in-command to Weizmann, a role he also performed for Simon at Marks and Spencer and one which he always claimed best-suited his temperament and talents. More accurately, Israel enjoyed playing the power-broker. False modesty aside, he knew just how much could be achieved from a position one step behind the front-man.

By the end of the war I was seeing the Weizmanns so frequently that I was treated as one of the family. When Weizmann's war work – his skills as a scientist were put at the disposal of the Admiralty – brought them to London, I often visited them at their flat in Camden Hill Road and later at the house in Addison Crescent. There were shared holidays, too, at a Jewish boarding-house in Blackpool for which my enthusiasm was muted by the bullying of the two Weizmann boys. Younger but stronger than I, they regarded these excursions as the open season for girl-baiting.

Weizmann himself was always very kind to me, taking time to promote intellectual curiosity. This was not done in any hectoring way, but rather as a good teacher relates to a pupil, picking up on questions to develop a theme but always leaving scope for more questions. Of Vera, his wife, I was not so sure. Unlike Chaim, whose family in Poland had been ensnared by the usual political and social restraints, Vera was of the privileged minority who succeeded in playing the Czarist ruling class at its own game. Her father rose from the conscripted ranks to become a general. His military experience evidently broadened his horizons, for when he retired from the army to set up a wholesaling business he determined on a Western European education for his daughter. Vera went to Geneva to study medicine, where she met Chaim who was teaching at the university.

The attraction between them supported the old theory of the marital compatibility of opposites. Though inseparable, there was always a distinction between the common-sense, down-to-earth Chaim and the aloof Vera. As a young girl I was made nervous by her easy assumption of superiority. There was something in her grand manner which always made me think twice about choosing the correct knife and fork.

The habit of lodging out – on relatives more often than on friends like the Weizmanns – became a regular way of life after Mother's death in 1917. I cannot pretend that her passing was of devastating impact. I was upset, of course, but the expectation of the event did much to cushion the blow. I may even have had a feeling of release since the ties that held me to what was left of my parents' home were regarded by me, quite wrongly I'm sure, as an unjust restraint.

I had long cherished a hope that I would be sent to boarding-school for the last years of my education. Now, it seemed, my ambition might be realized. Becky, however, had other ideas. A domestic solution was favoured whereby I was shunted from the Marks to the Sieffs to the Sachers and back again at three- to four-monthly intervals. Tilly,

MD—C

meanwhile, moved south to live with a family in Kent.

Though Becky could be a hard taskmaster, my best times were spent with her and Israel at their home at Didsbury. Their passion for politics and business made for a heady mix of visiting personalities whose conversation left me in a state of bewildered admiration. Yet, after all these years, it is not so much the deep thoughts and witty repartee that has remained with me, but more the idiosyncrasies of the individual guests.

How strange that Nahum Sokolow, scholar, writer and, by repute, an impeccable linguist, should with me always commit some transformation of English which left me flummoxed.

'Why does he call me "Kitchen"?' I asked Becky. She told me I had misheard.

'I'm sure I'm right,' I insisted, 'Next time, you listen.'

She did and was forced to agree. We puzzled about it for a long time before Becky came up with an answer: 'Of course, he means to call you "Chicken"!' That was at least understandable – 'Chicken' was then a common term of endearment – but the similarity between Kitchen and Chicken escaped me. Perhaps the confusion was in Polish or one of the other languages professed by Mr Sokolow.

Notable for eccentric behaviour was the extraordinary Professor Alexander, the philosopher friend of Arthur James Balfour, a luminary of the university and an authority on detective thrillers, which he devoured at the rate of one a day. It was he who came to dinner with his pyjama trousers underneath his dinner jacket. I knew because I could see an inch of striped material overlapping his shoes. But why? Was the archetypal academic so absent-minded as to overlay one set of clothes with another? Yet it seemed unlikely that he would be in night wear when he dressed for dinner. Anyway, this was not an isolated aberration. Perhaps he was subject to unpredictable fits of tiredness and needed to be prepared for a quick getaway to bed. Possible, but not probable, I decided. In the end, I swept prudence aside. I had to know. 'Please, would you mind telling me,' I muttered, 'why . . .'

'To keep warm,' he snapped. There was no answer to that.

Alexander was instrumental in renewing the acquaintance between Weizmann and Balfour. They had first met in 1906 when Balfour, Member for East Manchester, was fighting his first and last election as Prime Minister. Though swept out of office and out of Manchester in the Liberal landslide, Balfour took with him a fascination with Zionism as a bold and imaginative venture and a lasting impression of Weizmann as a politician deserving respect. When they met again, Balfour was back in power, only this time as Foreign Secretary in the Lloyd George wartime government.

By now the prospects for a Jewish national home had advanced significantly. Anglo-French deliberations on the future of Palestine once it had been wrested from Turkish suzerainty made honourable allowance for Jewish resettlement. The upshot was the Balfour Declaration, which viewed 'with favour the establishment in Palestine of a National Home for the Jewish people' (though not *the* National Home as Weizmann had wanted) and promised the government's 'best endeavours' to achieve this objective.

A few weeks later, the Turks were finally driven out of Palestine leaving the British, led by General Allenby, in uneasy control. The chances of another conflict if Arabs and Jews took up a nationalistic stance towards each other, occurred to politicians in London as readily as to the military on the spot. To pre-empt a crisis the government agreed to send a Zionist Commission to Palestine to forge 'friendly relations between the Jews on the one hand and the Arabs and non-Jewish communities on the other'. Weizmann was put at the head of the Commission of seven Jewish dignitaries, including a Frenchman and an Italian who were avowed anti-Zionists. Israel Sieff went along as secretary.

Israel's appointment, though a matter of some pride in the family, was mental torture for Becky, who saw it as her natural right to be at the centre of the action. Letters home detailing Israel's adventures merely added fuel to her frustration. She bubbled away for eight months until Israel's return, which coincided with the ending of the war in Europe. The pressure was then put on in earnest for him to share the limelight.

The Zionist Commission, meanwhile, was at a critical stage of its work. While the peace negotiator all but formally awarded the British the mandate for Palestine, this was not enough to ensure Weizmann and his colleagues a steady progression towards their goal. Relations with the Arabs, who felt let down by British and French double-talk, were close to breaking-point. There were disagreements within the government in London where the anti-Zionist Lord Curzon had succeeded Balfour as Foreign Secretary. To cap it all, a particularly fierce outbreak of anti-Semitism in the Ukraine was acting as a boost to immigration, which the Foreign Office was determined to resist.

When Israel went back to Palestine in 1920, Becky was with him. They were accompanied by an eighteen-year-old girl fresh out of school.

Learning By Experience

Palestine was my first experience of the outside world. I could have wished for a gentler initiation. The journey started promisingly with the boat train to Paris and, after a pause to take in the sights, a run across Europe to southern Italy. It was there that I fell victim to exotic cooking and primitive hygiene. On the boat to Alexandria I went down with an unnamed disease, which caused my guardians to exchange nervous glances, and in Cairo I was devoured by mosquitoes slowly and with relish as if I were some rare delicacy.

For the last leg of the journey, from Cairo to Palestine, we boarded the 'milk-and-honey express'. Notwithstanding my frailties, I took encouragement from the name of the conveyance. But like so much else in that part of the world, it was an illusion, at best an attempt at heavy irony. The milk-and-honey express was a long convoy of roughly converted freight cars, dragged along by an elderly locomotive. The 'express', I need hardly add, moved very slowly.

The resolution of Becky and Israel in the face of man-made adversity was amazing to see. They took it all in the spirit of true pioneers. Becky did her best to encourage me. 'Think of it as part of your education,' she said.

I was given more than a hint of what was to come when the train dropped us off at Lod, ten miles out of Tel Aviv. Where today there is a busy international airport, the only sign of occupation was a canvas lean-to at the side of the track. A little way off was parked an army car, which looked as if it had done sterling service during the war. A young officer came forward to greet us – politely but formally. Then we all piled into the car and set off.

Negotiating the road reminded me of progress on a snakes and ladders board – two moves forward and one back. The penalty squares were the potholes. Avoiding them must have added several miles to the journey, but a circuitous route was better than getting

27

a puncture or a broken axle. I did not fancy being stranded in the desert.

'Is all of Palestine like this?' I asked Becky.

'Not all,' she said, 'but most of it.'

The drive into Tel Aviv was like riding into a Wild West shanty town – on early closing day. Tel Aviv, or the Hill of the Spring (another example of Jewish irony), was two rows of buildings divided by a single dusty street. But it was at least an entirely Jewish settlement, an outpost of Zionism, all of ten years old, where we were sure to receive an enthusiastic welcome. A house was made available for us to stay in for a few days while Israel and Becky met with community leaders.

While Israel and Becky talked, I listened. Peppered by conflicting views, I began to realize that Zionism was by no means a clear-cut political philosophy. The achievement of a national home was the ideal, but to define its structure and purpose within the complex jigsaw of Middle East politics was a fearful challenge few were able to meet.

I acquired a clearer appreciation of the issues, if not of their resolution, when we moved on to Jerusalem, the headquarters of the British administration. Everyone seemed to be playing a double game. The occupying power, hooked on contradictory promises to Jews and Arabs, expressed sympathy for Zionism while trying hard to bury it. Except in private conversations the Balfour Declaration was never mentioned. I was told later by Harry Sacher that the actual document was kept in a file marked secret. This, however, was not enough to reconcile the Arabs, who could not quite decide if the Jews were agents of European imperialism or political allies against foreign rule.

The Jews themselves added to the confusion by failing to make clear what they wanted in Palestine. Was *a* national home to become *the* national home. If yes, was the national home to evolve into an independent state? The difficulty of answering these questions was compounded by the overlap between genuine conviction and political tactics. Weizmann, for example, had a vision of a fully fledged Jewish nation, of making Palestine, as he put it, 'as Jewish as England is English'. Yet he was also a gradualist who looked to future generations to fulfil his dream. At least, that is what he told British politicians, who found it impossible to distinguish between Weizmann the single-minded nationalist and Weizmann the supreme diplomat.

Becky rescued me from confusion with her clear-cut notions of a Jewish nation in the making. We were not, as some anti-Zionists suggested, usurpers of Arab property. The Jews, though a minority, had every right to stake a claim in what after all was a territory without any clear sense of purpose or identity. The problem was to make our presence felt in a constructive way.

While Israel battled away as Weizmann's representative on the Zionist Commission (the leader himself was better occupied advancing the cause among opinion leaders in Paris and London), Becky kept up a punishing routine as a peripatetic social worker. When a school was to be erected, Becky went along to advise on amenities; when a hospital was to be opened, Becky somehow found money for badly needed drugs and equipment; and when there was evidence of hardship and suffering, Becky took the lead in bullying the civil servants into action.

Conditions were uniformly primitive. Jerusalem had no electricity, nor even a regular water supply. Though Israel and Becky eventually managed to rent a half-decent house, in the short period I was with them we were accommodated in the Russian Compound, a vast, ugly fortress of a building which incorporated the city prison. The only alternative was a tenth-rate hotel known as The Allenby, a dubious compliment to the general who had masterminded the Turkish defeat.

In the first few weeks we were urged to restrict our movements, particularly after dark. Attacks on two Jewish settlements in the north had been followed by riots in Jerusalem, and trigger-happy robbers were said to be roaming the streets. This did not stop me getting out to the numerous dances and parties hosted by Allenby's younger staff officers. With a military escort, I knew no fear. Alone, however, my security was easily shattered. Returning to my room one night, I was struggling with the paraffin lamp when I heard a movement. As the blue light flared up, there was a wild scampering towards me, a chair crashed over and I screamed. I kept on screaming even after I caught the unmistakable sight and smell of a mangy dog in full flight. The sense of relief, when it did come, was diminished by the sure knowledge that I had panicked the wretched beast into relieving itself on my bed.

29

The excitement and interest of Palestine was greater in retrospect as, when returning to Manchester, I was able to recount my adventures to friends and family. I realized then that without thinking very positively about it, I had caught some part of the spirit of Zionism – a longing for achievement, perhaps, or, to reveal the other face of the same coin, an impatience with inactivity. It was the frustration of energy that I most resented in Palestine where the British interpretation of responsibility was 'not wishing to upset nurse for fear of getting something worse'. It was a policy, I believed, which was bound to lead to failure and humiliation. It was not for me. I wanted to get things done.

With Becky's prolonged absence, my homes in Manchester were reduced to two: the Sachers and the Marks. As Harry Sacher was also determined to do his share in Palestine (he was to practise as a lawyer there for nine years), I knew that before long I would be seeing an awful lot of Simon and Miriam. Though slightly nervous at the prospect of binding myself so closely to an elder brother with whom I did not always see eye to eye, I confess to a feeling of relief at escaping from the Sacher household. Harry was always quick to show irritation which annoyed me and so made him yet more bad-tempered. It was as if we both had a deep-rooted desire to get on each other's nerves. Matters came to a head one weekend when Miriam, who had bronchitis, was away on one of her frequent excursions to the warm south coast. I joined Harry and a few of his friends for lunch, but after the meal I left them talking while I went upstairs to read. Some time later I returned to find Harry seated alone at the table. He gave me a glare. 'You couldn't even take the trouble to close the door. I've been sitting in a draught for three hours.'

I started cautiously, but ended up on a high shout: 'Can't you do anything for yourself? You're not so important you have to be waited on hand and foot. If you wanted the door closed, why didn't you get up and close it?'

He did not speak to me again for a week. Victory! But there was a further drama to come. A short time afterwards, I went down with a bad attack of diphtheria. In the absence of both Miriam and Harry, a friend called the doctor who packed me off to bed. To break the fever, I needed a vaccine, but since the risks of failure were high I also needed permission from a close relative for the medical prescription to go ahead. Eventually, Simon was alerted by a station appeal which he heard as he got off the train at Euston. I was saved.

Harry, meanwhile, remained in ignorance of the domestic trauma until he arrived home to find his sister-in-law under the blankets, a nurse in attendance and a disinfected sheet hanging over the doorway to bar his entrance to the sick-room. I am delighted to record that he was thoroughly shocked and suffered a bad conscience for at least a month. After that we started rowing again.

Moving in with Simon and Miriam on a more or less permanent basis brought home to me a fact of life which up to then I had taken for granted. The rise of Marks and Spencer had made me a young lady of independent and comfortable means. For this I had Simon to thank. His genius for managing a complex and high-risk business had transformed the modest fortune left by my father and shared equally between his children into a very substantial fortune indeed.

By the early 1920s, the Marks and Spencer store was a familiar sight in high streets throughout the country. They were usually accommodated in premises more substantial and spacious than those associated with the old Penny Bazaars. A policy of abandoning the open stalls in favour of shops with proper fronts and window displays was well under way before the end of the war. To attract passers-by, there was renewed emphasis on attractive presentation which favoured long, wide counters and bright lights. Once in, customers were welcomed by neatly dressed assistants, who were taught to be polite and cheerful – even on Mondays.

The new 'family' stores carried a much wider range of products at a much wider range of prices. The demise of the penny-only policy caused by wartime inflation (a shocking occurrence for a society used to an entirely stable currency) turned out to be a blessing in disguise. It enabled Marks and Spencer to extend its appeal to the young middle class, the families who were sufficiently affluent to put down a £50 deposit for a new semi on the arterial road. A top price of 5/- was adopted with the promise that most items on display should sell at around 1/-. Signifying quality at reasonable prices, Marks and Spencer had a powerful attraction for those who nowadays would be called the upwardly mobile.

F.W. Woolworth, meanwhile, went down-market with its reputation, doggedly preserved, as the 3d and 6d store. Imaginative efforts were made to accommodate the general rise in prices. For a short while, I recall, the more expensive range of Woolworth's footwear was sold at 6d a shoe, while a pair of spectacles cost, in reality, 18d – 6d for the frame and 6d each for the lenses.

With the expansion of Marks and Spencer came a shift of power-base from Manchester to London. The capital was the centre of all that was new and exciting in mass retailing. Simon could reel off the names of his competitors – Debenham and Freebody, Marshall and Snelgrove, Peter Robinson, Bourne and Hollingsworth, Swan and Edgar, John Lewis and, above all, Selfridge's. Gordon Selfridge from Chicago had built the biggest department store in Britain, which Simon called 'a people's palace'. He greatly admired the Selfridge flair for publicity and for eye-catching displays. Where else would you see store windows illuminated until midnight?

In 1924 the Marks and Spencer head office moved to Chiswell Street close to the City. Four years later, after the company had gone public, new and larger premises close by were christened Michael House. But yet again Marks and Spencer outgrew its home. In 1931 Michael House moved to Baker Street, where it remains to this day.

In skipping lightly over the early years of the company's history, I must not give the impression of an easy and inexorable rise to greatness. In the critical period immediately following the war, the aspect of growth which preoccupied Simon was the size of the bank overdraft. While committed to investment in modern stores as the only way forward, he was apprehensive of an all-out battle for high-street dominance with contenders like Woolworth, who were capable of deploying substantial financial reserves.

In 1924 Simon went to the United States, the mecca for ambitious retailers, where he gave himself a crash course in advanced store management. He came back full of the wonders of American skills in stock control, automatic accounting and marketing. One of his first moves was to introduce a sophisticated system of stock-check lists which determined the flow of goods from factory to stores. Conventional shopkeepers thought it all a great waste of time until they saw what a difference it made to the profit margin.

In the odd moments when Simon was not running the company, he gave thought to the future of his youngest sister. I was at a difficult age, difficult that is for everyone except Elaine. For the life of me I could not understand what all the fuss was about. In my own estimation I was sensible, level-headed and well able to take care of my own best interests. If this judgement were open to bias, so also was Simon's assessment of me as a confused romantic who was likely to rush off with the first fortune-hunter who managed to get his toe in the door. Boys who showed more than a passing interest were put through a rigorous interrogation. Even when they were proved free of pecuniary motives (most seemed to have more than enough money of their own), they were liable to be voted down on other grounds of unsuitability, of which there were many. Simon was a very hard man to please.

One who failed to pass muster was Neville Blond. 'Why?' I demanded to know.

'I don't want to discuss it,' said Simon.

The mystery of Neville's ineligibility was made all the greater by his friendship with Simon. I could only think that my brother's judgement was swayed by envy. Perhaps he saw in Neville a capacity for enjoying life which he could never hope to share. Unflattering comments, to others, about Neville's adventures in Paris, where for three years after the war he had sown an acreage of wild oats, were later relayed to me as a more rational explanation for Simon's intransigence. But Simon was quite capable of disguising his fear of being upstaged. Prudery is ever the mask of jealousy.

The irony in all this was that Neville would have done anything to avoid offending Simon. He was a devotee of the Marks and Spencer enterprise, and at the time when he and his brother Horace were setting up their own textile business, Neville looked to Simon as the entrepreneurial leader of his generation.

There were many years to roll by before Neville and I could talk openly about such matters. Despite all that has been said about the madcap 1920s, family institutions were still powerful enough to quash an unwelcome romance. I met with Neville quite frequently, but always in company and never in circumstances that were other than perfectly respectable.

Meanwhile, I was being gently edged towards the officially approved candidate for my affections. Norman Laski, a cousin of Neville's whose mother was a Laski, was close to the power centre of Manchester Jewry. His uncle, Nathan Laski, was, in his own estimation, the leader of the Jewish community. No one was prepared to argue with him. His authority was not dependent on great wealth, though he made more than a comfortable income as a middleman in the cotton trade between Lancashire and India. Rather, his ascendancy derived from an indefatigable desire to have the last word.

This was made evident by the events leading to the erection of the Jewish hospital in Elizabeth Street. It was a project which Nathan opposed with all his strength. He saw it as an attempt to segregate Jews in a way that was socially harmful. A happier alternative, he believed, was to enhance the appeal of the general hospital, but his only suggestion for achieving this was to open a kosher restaurant next door, an idea which seemed not to measure up to the seriousness of the issue. Eventually, he gave way with as much good grace as he could muster and the hospital was built. A humiliating defeat, everyone believed. But no. As soon as the red tape was cut, Nathan got himself drafted on to the management committee. A few years later he was made president and became so closely involved in the affairs of the hospital that it was said he often accompanied doctors on their rounds of the wards and was not above proclaiming the occasional diagnosis. It was no surprise to me when, recently, the hospital was closed to hear that one of the last items to be removed was a life-sized portrait of Nathan. Apparently, they had great difficulty in getting it out of the door.

Norman's parents were no less confident of their superiority, but circumstances made them less obtrusive. Having decided at an early age that he was suffering from consumption, Norman's father gave up work to concentrate on his round of visits to doctors and sanatoriums. He spent a lot of time in Switzerland breathing mountain air. This presumably did him good, since whenever we met he always seemed to be in the peak of fitness. A small, dapper man, he walked very quickly tapping out his steps with a silver-topped cane. My daughter Ann nicknamed him Felix because he reminded her of the cartoon cat, who, in his signature tune, 'went on walking, walking'. Norman's mother was strict, unforgiving and easily slighted. As each of her numerous sisters had given her cause for offence, she never spoke to any of them. To me, she was considerate if never affectionate. I felt I could adjust to my parents-in-law as long as they rationed their visits, which they were willing to do. Absence makes the heart more tolerant.

My relationship with Nathan was quite a different matter. From the very beginning it was clear that we would not get along. We disagreed on every likely topic of discussion from Zionism (he was against it) to feminism (he was against that too). He had a daughter, Mabel, who was mis-shaped into a permanent crouch, but who deflected any sympathy with an acid tongue. Miriam said of her that she was stunted in mind and body. Nathan also had two clever sons: Neville, who, inheriting his father's domineering spirit, took naturally to the law (he ended his days as Recorder of Liverpool with a reputation for handing down stiff sentences), and Harold, the black sheep of the family.

Harold married a Christian, professed atheism but, most shocking of all, became a socialist and, since Nathan's side of the family never did anything by halves, a leading left-wing socialist at that. During my acclimatization to Laski family rituals, Harold was not much in evidence. His re-entry to the dinner circle had to wait until he achieved respectability of sorts as Professor of Political Science at the London School of Economics. By then he was a national figure with a string of books, articles and polemics to his name.

When my engagement to Norman was announced, we did make a point of going to see cousin Harold. The conversation was formal, but, in the absence of anyone to offer us a drink, mercifully short. As we departed, Harold slapped Norman on the back. 'Good luck. You have a lot to look forward to. With your love of cricket and Elaine's passion for Zionism, you could end up as captain of the Palestinian Eleven!' You might gather from this that the family did not regard Norman as a potential high-flyer.

They were right, of course. And, I must quickly add, I do not believe I was ever under any illusions. One reason why we were so wrapped up with Nathan and his affairs was that Norman was too self-effacing to do other than defer to the great man. But what was seen as weakness by the forceful Laskis had a distinct appeal for me. Norman was kind, gentle and considerate. When the children came along he was the model father. Oh yes, given a free hand, I would have chosen a more dashing figure as the ideal husband – Neville Blond was never far from my thoughts – but within the confines of Simon's dictate, Norman offered the only practical escape route into adulthood. Whenever there were doubts, I took strength from the thought that soon I would be able to handle my own life in my own way. This is what I was telling myself right up to the last moment when in a crowded synagogue Norman and I were standing before the rabbi waiting for our cue to exchange rings. My sister Miriam knew well enough what was going on in my mind. 'Elaine is looking the wrong way!' she murmured to her neighbour, when at a critical point in the service my eyes were diverted towards the best man. It was the way he stood looking straight ahead with shoulders back, his hands clasped behind him; the civilian clothes could not disguise the military bearing. There was no doubt about it, Neville Blond was very handsome.

The first night of the honeymoon was spent in Liverpool, not the most romantic of settings but one which seemed preferable to the suggested alternative, the overnight sleeper to London. Instead, it was agreed that we should travel the following day. The purpose of the journey was to join a P & O liner bound for India where, taking advantage of business connections, we were to embark on a two-month tour.

The appeal of this adventure was dampened somewhat by worries over administrative details. Once the confusion about first-night accommodation was cleared up, I found that our train ticket only entitled us to a second-class compartment ('Oh, no, not on my honeymoon').

Then there was the more serious problem of dealing with Nathan. He came along to the station to wish us well. There was no harm in that, although I was perturbed to discover that he was also on his way to London; I was more concerned still to find him at the dock waiting to embark us on our ship. He was with us for the entire expedition.

In fairness, I should have known. Nathan was an annual visitor to India, where the major part of his business, the sale of cotton fabrics, was located. It was asking too much of his nature to assume that he could pass up the opportunity of educating his nephew, now employed by the family firm, in the finer points of the textile trade. As for bothering to consult me before making his plans, well, that too was unthinkable.

And so we fought and argued our way round the subcontinent. The talk was mostly about Zionism and the future of the Jewish homeland. In crowded trains (where our debates constituted a popular spectator sport), hotel lobbies and open cars we bandied great thoughts and stronger principles with Norman performing the thankless task of umpire. In retrospect, I must be grateful for an excellent training in the art of disputation. Nathan was a powerful advocate of his beliefs and so made me examine all the harder the justice of my own cause. Where I think I won points (no doubt if Nathan was here to comment he would disagree profoundly) was in detecting a contradiction in his wish to retain the Jewish identity without the commitment to a Jewish home.

'How is that possible?' I demanded to know. 'If we abandon Palestine, what guarantee can there be that our identity will survive?'

Nathan was ready for that: 'The Jews have overcome many hardships. They will survive.'

'But on what terms? Do you call the Pale of Settlement survival? Where is the pride in poverty and degradation? You think only of your own example. You've done well in a country which is sympathetic to Jews. But suppose you had been brought up in Russia? You might now be praying for escape to a Jewish homeland, as your only hope!'

It was an unkind cut, for Nathan had been born in Russia and might well have stayed there but for his father, who had the foresight to get his family out before the climax of the pogroms. However, Nathan was not to be swayed by memories of his own lucky release.

'The Jews can best protect their identity by integrating with their adopted societies, not by setting up in rivalry with them!' Impasse!

Absorbed by Jewish nationalism, I was neither surprised nor disturbed to detect a strong Indian sentiment in favour of independence. To those Indians we saw demonstrating in the streets against the British Raj I was inclined to say 'Good Luck'. My male companions, who judged events through business eyes, took a less sanguine view. India was by far the biggest market for British cotton goods, but it was a market which was highly susceptible to domestic competition. After all, India produced her own raw cotton, so manufacturing could just as easily be carried out at home as in Lancashire. In fact, more easily. It was only the imperial tradition which dictated otherwise and already, even at this early stage of the independence movement, the imperialists looked to be in headlong retreat.

Our Indian journey took place in 1924. In the preceding decade, we learned, the import of cotton goods from Lancashire had fallen by over fifty per cent. Our hosts, mostly wealthy merchants whose own livelihood was at stake, tried hard to persuade us that the trend was reversible. If manufacturing costs were to be reduced by greater efficiency and more effort was put into selling (how often were we to hear of these palliatives over the years?), then Lancashire could hold on to her market share and maybe even make up some lost ground. But the Laskis remained sceptical. Even if we could overturn convention, we still had to counter the nationalist objection to buying British.

Listening to the devotees of Mahatma Gandhi, whose recent spell in prison had only served to enhance his reputation for saintly forbearance, it was almost possible to believe that Indian nationalists were granting a favour by depriving Lancashire of employment. In any event, this was precisely what they did. By 1930 our cotton exports to India had been halved yet again.

But my honeymoon was entirely devoted to business and politics. We were entertained royally and shown the sights in grand style.

From Bombay we progressed north to Delhi and then on to Kashmir, where we viewed the Himalayas and were taken on a pony trek over what I was assured were the lower foothills. The views were inspiring, the heights terrifying and regard for safety non-existent. Our guide said that he had taken the same route many times before and had never had an accident. There must have been some fundamental difference in our philosophies on life which made me accept, and him disbelieve, that there could be a first time.

In Srinagar, the summer capital, we dined with a retired army officer who lived on a houseboat, one of hundreds which crowded the river banks. It was a spacious and comfortable residence, a Noah's Ark lookalike, with accommodation for numerous servants and a most impressive kitchen (or galley?) where delectable Persian dishes were cooked in a clay stove. Captivated by what at first I assumed to be our host's declaration of individuality, I soon found out that his style of living was quite customary for the long-term English residents. It was the only way they had of circumventing the maharajah's ruling that no foreigner should own *land* in Kashmir.

Over time, impressions merge: the sumptuous colours and cool fountains of the Shalimar, the Moghul garden beside which pale hands were loved; the first clear glimpse of Everest, a hundred miles to the north of where we stayed in Darjeeling; the temples and bazaars of Delhi; and the almost completed construction of New Delhi, the latest seat of government, with its spacious avenues and cleanly defined buildings, the Welwyn Garden City of the Orient.

At the Taj Mahal, as much a symbol of India as the Eiffel Tower is of France, I could not help reflecting that one of the great architectural wonders of the world is, in fact, a tomb, and that so much had been lavished on a dedication to the dead while outside in the dusty roads the beggars were starving.

This ever present distinction between flamboyant wealth and abject poverty was distressing and sometimes obscene. Staying at the Taj Mahal – the Bombay hotel not the memorial – I was woken by what sounded like the rustling of a thousand newspapers. I discovered later that it was the sound of the rats scavenging on the docks. By day I had seen the street dwellers there, also scavenging.

It has to be said for the Indians that they were at least open about their poverty. Perhaps they had no choice. The scale of deprivation was such as to forbid dissembling. Still, I gave them credit for not even trying to imitate the European custom of hiding the destitute in dark corners. What I could not forgive was the apparent indifference to poverty. Both Indians and their British overlords seemed to regard it as part of the natural order. There were times when I could have screamed with frustration. In Calcutta I saw ragged children, each clutching a tin mug, waiting in line before a boiling cauldron to receive what I assumed to be hot soup. It was actually hot water they were getting – a whole cupful each. At least they could be sure that it was not contaminated, unlike the water most of the street urchins were forced to drink.

When I asked to see more of Calcutta I was taken in an open car to view the bazaars. A less appropriate conveyance it is difficult to imagine. In the narrow streets we advanced at a snail's pace against a tide of humanity. It was hopeless. I was better off walking, which I insisted on doing. Clasping my wide-brimmed hat and gathering my skirts, I led the way into the labyrinth. I felt like one of those men who used to carry a red flag in front of motor vehicles – though I doubt that they ever encountered my problem, which was to walk too fast for the car to keep up. I turned round and the car was not there.

With a tremor of panic, I started back the way I had come. Still no car. There was only one thing to do: I had to ask help. But whom? With the crush of bodies around me, I was spoilt for choice. Yet there was no gainsaying my fear of approaching someone, who, finding I was alone and lost, might want to harm me: I took the plunge. He was a businessman, I guessed, taller than the average and very imposing with his white kulla flowing down to his shoes.

'Please . . . would you mind . . . I seem to be lost . . . can you tell me . . . my car . . .'

I am sure I barely made sense, but the response was immediate. My appeal was passed on to others in the crowd. Suddenly, the people who had been pushing, shouting, intent above all on the quick sale, became friendly, eager to help, infinitely courteous. We found the car two streets away. I thanked everyone profusely. Should I tip? I gave some money to children, which appeared to meet with approval. No doubt they thought I was a foolish Englishwoman. I am sure they laughed at my ineptitude and needless fears. They had every right. But on my part there was nothing but gratitude, not simply for the practical assistance but for the initiation to the true India. I was no longer frightened.

I did have some hard words for my driver, as he had not even noticed that I was missing.

For the journey home Nathan and I agreed on a truce. He kept his distance and I kept my temper. The three weeks at sea were quiet and restful.

The Wider World

Back in England, I immediately started looking around for something to do. I did not want to follow in the wake of my elder sister, but Becky was so fiendishly active that it was difficult not to fall under her influence.

The ruling forces in her life were Zionism and feminism. The family came third. I know the reaction this gets from people who never knew Becky. How selfish, how unfeeling! But suppose we were talking about a man. Ah, that would be different as, of course, it *is* different for nearly all top businessmen and politicians. The double standard infuriated Becky. She was not the sort of person to allow ambition to be smothered by convention. Israel accepted her point of view – perhaps he had little choice – but while both were accustomed to go their own way, the bond between them was stronger than in most marriages I have known.

The vehicles for Becky's assault on male dominance were two organizations which she was instrumental in founding. The Federation of Women Zionists (FWZ) was an amalgam of various charitable enterprises linked to the Jewish community in Palestine. It was set up shortly after the war to 'promote the welfare of Jewish women and children in Palestine' and 'to foster Jewish national consciousness among the Jewish women of the United Kingdom'. As sister of the first president of the FWZ I was one of the early victims of her determination, which she had written into the constitution, to recreate Hebrew as 'a living language'.

The FWZ was an undoubted success in spreading the word and raising funds. But in terms of real influence in the higher councils of Zionism, the ladies were, at best, treated with polite condescension. Becky needed a stronger power-base. In June 1920 she led the call for a Women's International Conference. It was held a month later in London at the Russell Hotel, where Becky made the speech of a lifetime, calling upon her audience to face up to the challenge of creating a Jewish national home as they would to a holy crusade. The mood of euphoria inspired by Becky overcame the doubters who feared upsetting the establishment and carried the delegates through to an overwhelming vote for a Women's International Zionist Organization, henceforth to be known as WIZO.

In the first heady weeks Becky spoke at meetings up and down the country, appealing on behalf of women and children in Palestine, many of them recent immigrants, who were suffering appalling deprivation. The response was immediate and generous. But the very success of the early WIZO campaign created an embarrassing overlap between Becky's national and international interests. As a leading figure in both the FWZ and WIZO she was not at first conscious of the problem. But those who worked for one or the other or, more to the point, were not sure who they were working for, eventually raised their voices in protest. A formal division of responsibilities was agreed with Becky invariably choosing to wear her WIZO hat.

At the Manchester end I was naturally recruited for donkey work on the fund-raising front. Even if Becky was off on her travels, the two Miriams – my sister and sister-in-law – were ever ready to remind me of my duty. They even made formal recognition of my contribution: I was elected chairman of the Didsbury branch of FWZ. However, I made strenuous efforts to extend my social activities beyond the family circle.

The obvious solution was to take up visiting. Among the wives of Didsbury, the fashionable middle-class suburb where Norman and I made our first home, it was customary to spend one or two afternoons visiting the poor. No doubt they meant well, as I did, but amateurish attempts to illuminate the gloomier districts of Manchester were not well received. The help given was modest and the terms on which it was given – a cosy homily on the need for hard work and frugal living – were intolerable for people already at the end of their tether. I tried to think of more practical ways of breaking the poverty cycle.

The most sensible proposal, I believed, came from another resident of Manchester, the author of two best-sellers, *Married Love* and *Wise Parenthood*, and the leading exponent of birth control. Dr Marie Stopes was a brilliant scientist though not a medical doctor. She knew more about the constitution of coal (for which she received international recognition) than the constitution of the human body. But an unconsummated marriage (as much a consequence of Marie's early innocence, we were given to understand, as of her husband's inability) inspired in her the need to educate and inform.

Her appeal for those of us who wanted, in some small way, to change society was in the hope of persuading poorer families that frequent procreation was not a burden allotted to them by divine providence. Unfortunately the message was not put across with sufficient clarity or determination. This was because Marie herself was not entirely clear as to what she wanted to achieve. Her advice on creating a loving relationship in marriage, for example, was smothered by a romantic sentiment more befitting a cheap novel.

In many respects, Marie was more the Victorian than the modern woman. Her maternal ideal was still the dedicated and self-sacrificing homemaker, an image which did not accord with feminist views, even if it helped to reassure some faint hearts in public life. There were even a few doctors who came over to our side, though the medical profession as a whole remained hostile as did the Roman Catholic church. Both had a vested interest in boundless fertility.

Marie Stopes's first birth-control clinic was set up in London in 1921. It had a slow start – working-class women were chary of seeking advice on a subject which they could barely bring themselves to discuss with their own husbands. But strenuous opposition from moralists helped to publicize her views. In Manchester, the feminist movement was quick to respond. Meetings were organized and a decision made: we were to have our own birth-control clinic.

A leading light in the makeshift organization was Dr Edith Summerskill, already a tough and determined fighter for just causes. Another was Mary Stocks, daughter of an enlightened GP and wife of an equally enlightened academic who was to become principal of Westfield College in London. We were not short on sound, practical common sense.

Our consulting rooms were ideally placed in at least two respects. They were in the heart of an overcrowded working-class district and they were over a pie shop. This second feature proved invaluable in attracting shy clients, who could pretend to inquisitive passers-by that they were ordinary shoppers. Our drawback was the large Roman Catholic church just down the road. The priest and his elders did all they could to frustrate our activities, even to the extent of organizing a none-too-peaceful demonstration. We demanded, and got, police protection.

Whenever we had the chance to explain our belief we made clear our dedication to family planning – having children when you wanted them – not family prevention. Yet our opponents could only see us as the enemies of the family, promoters of licentiousness, even as abortionists. A Roman Catholic journal described us as 'the kind of idle women who visit matinees and sit with cigarettes between their painted lips'. The truth, at least in my case, was more mundane. I was the sort of woman who, being heavily pregnant with my first child, spent more time advising on how to have babies than on how not to have them. Thankfully, I never had to go into details. There was always a female doctor and two nurse midwives on hand to give professional judgement.

In terms of practical help our contribution was small. Those who attribute the lower birth rate to Marie Stopes's ladies should be reminded that the trend was there in the 1890s. But as part of the wider feminist movement we did make a start in changing man's conception of woman, even perhaps of woman's conception of herself.

Though reputed to be years of social upheaval the 1920s were, in fact, deeply conservative in all except feminism. This was the only genuine revolution. And because the women's cause was so successful in breaking the taboos of politics, education and employment, we were the natural target of abuse for the diehards – our self-appointed male guardians who, when faced with a challenge, could only respond by promoting the sanctity of convention.

For now, most of my battles with the old guard were within the family – Nathan Laski still the prime target. The nadir of our relationship came at a family dinner, where the main topic of conversation was the suitability of a proposed marriage partner for one of Norman's cousins. The poor woman, who was not present to speak in her defence, was criticized on almost every count, including financial.

'Wouldn't you think Horace could do better for himself?' asked Nathan before declaring his own verdict. 'The girl has no breeding.'

I snapped. 'Is that all you care about, breeding? I'm surprised I'm good enough for you. Is this how you talked about me before I married Norman?'

The long silence was answer enough. I got up and walked out of the house. Norman came on later making apologies.

'There's only one person who should apologize,' I shouted at him, 'and it's not you, and it's not me!' As a peacemaker, Norman got very little thanks.

In 1927 Ann was born and Norman was made a director of Marks and Spencer. (Simon was always keen to involve male relatives in the business.) This was also the year after the General Strike, an event which in itself made little impact on our lives but which came to symbolize what was apparent to all of us: the decay of the industrial north. As business drifted away, so the confidence and pride went out of Manchester. Like the other once great northern cities, it became drab and depressing. Instead of hope, there was only the expectation of worse to come.

While Norman adapted to Marks and Spencer I spent more time in London, usually staying with Simon and Miriam at their splendid house in Frognal. By now Marks and Spencer was a leading public company with over 200 stores. Of the £2 million turnover, about one quarter was pre-tax profit. Within ten years the turnover was to increase to £11 million and profits to £1 million – not bad for a recession.

Notwithstanding a large injection of capital from Prudential Assurance, Simon was still very much in charge. At his right hand was Israel Sieff, lately advanced to a full-time director and vice-chairman. Harry Sacher was also on the board. Family control was further protected by the policy of issuing shares without voting rights.

Counter gazing in one of the new Marks and Spencer superstores was in itself an antidote to recession. The range of goods had by now extended to clothes and food, two sales categories which were to become the leading revenue earners after 1930. Direct competition with the grocery and tailoring chains, who boasted their own standards of excellence, accentuated the need for quality control. Determined to do away with what he called 'hit and miss' methods of buying, Simon encouraged closer involvement with manufacturing. In this way, suppliers could take account of the precise requirements of Marks and Spencer at the critical planning stage of production. Advice even extended to the purchase of raw materials. As Israel told a meeting in 1931, helping manufacturers to get the best possible deal on their buying was entirely to the benefit of Marks and Spencer customers, who in consequence paid lower prices in the shops.

But it was not only the customers who saw in Marks and Spencer the bright side of the economy. For staff too, the present was more tolerable and the future entirely encouraging. The idea of caring for staff had been part of the Marks and Spencer management philosophy ever since the days when Simon had insisted that the counter girls 'needed a good meal to do the work properly'. It is true that by modern standards, stores in the 1920s left much to be desired. A former staffer at the Church Street store in Blackpool, who started there in 1923, recalls 'a small room used as a canteen, with one lav and a basin in the corner. This was used by all staff, and if someone pulled the chain you had to wait for the cistern to fill before you could get any water.'

At Kingsland Road in East London the male staff were given a weekly allowance of 1s 3d to use the nearby public lavatory. All this was soon to change, but it is worth remembering, in context, that the Blackpool Marks and Spencer could count itself unusual in having a canteen at all, however tiny. As for Kingsland Road, if it had been any other company, the pay packets would not have included what I suppose must be called inconvenience money. Conditions in what was traditionally a hard graft business were so much better in Marks and Spencer than in most other stores that very few of our employees ever wanted to leave.

Simon often referred to the 'sense of amity' characterizing staff relations. At an end of year celebration in 1923 he spoke proudly of seeing 'the same faces year after year', which suggested that 'people like us and like to remain our servants'. A touch patronizing perhaps, but the sentiment was genuine as it was when he described 'the enthusiasm, devotion and energy' of the Marks and Spencer staff as 'one of the main assets of the business'.

Staff services were upgraded in the early 1930s when head office took on direct responsibility for welfare and training and a Personnel Department was set up. Norman was its first director.

The leading light on his staff was Flora Solomon, the spinster daughter of a Russian banker who emigrated to the United States, made a vast fortune on Wall Street and lost it all in the 1931 crash. When her £1,000-a-month allowance dried up, Flora went out to look for a job. Her version of subsequent events starts at a dinner with Simon, when she told him that Marks and Spencer had 'a shrinking reputation for labour conditions'. Simon always denied this story.

He told me on more than one occasion that in his first conversation with Flora, it was clear that she knew next to nothing about Marks and Spencer. But she did show an interest in staff welfare and, since she was obviously in need of work, Simon decided to let her try her hand.

Once into the company she acted vigorously to give female staff a better deal. Her discovery that in some stores pregnant women were allowed to carry heavy packages, and that throughout Marks and Spencer pregnancy did not qualify for sick pay, alone justified the expense of setting up a welfare department.

Smarter and more spacious canteens, a medical service, and social and athletic clubs followed in profusion. A pension scheme (at first only for senior men, a bone of contention between Simon and the Marks sisters) was introduced in 1935. At the same time the family endowed a Marks and Spencer Benevolent Trust, which was supplemented annually from company profits.

Wages stayed well above average for the retail business but, yet more comfortingly, fear of unemployment was kept at bay. 'We have made it a duty', declared Simon, 'to keep on as many as possible. There are branches which we might have closed with profit, but we prefer to keep them going and so not add to the unemployment.'

Simon and Israel were infinitely proud of the family atmosphere they worked hard to create. Both put themselves out to make contact with the staff, which meant a lot of travelling, a willingness to listen and a capacity for always remaining cheerful. Simon had the most appalling temper, but this he reserved exclusively for his fellow directors and for the family. His employees saw only the gentle, caring side of his character. The supporting anecdotes are legion; one will suffice.

When a junior at head office stepped back from the lift in deference to Simon, he was told, 'Come in, you won't catch anything.' And when he got out, Simon called after him, 'Even if you do catch anything, we'll look after you.'

In 1930, three months after my second daughter Simone was born, we moved permanently to London. We were part of a middle-class exodus. It was amazing how often I met people in London whom I had previously assumed to be inveterate Mancunians. We all came down for the same reason: the opportunity to be at the centre of things, whether in business, politics or fashion.

47

Before leaving Manchester, I received another valuable object lesson in 'keeping calm in a crisis'. Glancing over a copy of the *Manchester Evening News*, my eyes caught and held by the headline 'SIEFF FAMILY MISSING'. The story of a boat lost in the Dead Sea. Becky, Israel and the children had been on board and they were feared drowned.

My first thought was to reach Simon, though what he could do to help was not immediately apparent. I rushed to the phone but while communicating, none too articulately I dare say, with a slow-witted operator, one of the maids appeared to find out what the fuss was about. I pointed to the paper, which she recovered from the floor and neatly refolded.

'Yes,' she said, smiling in a knowing sort of way, '*Isn't* it good news!'

'What did you say?' I began, furious now as well as frightened.

She was still smiling. 'It's all here, look!' She said pointing to a Stop Press item: 'SIEFF FAMILY FOUND – ALL SAFE'. Since then I have always read the newspaper from back to front.

Arriving in London, not as a visitor but as a resident, I was conscious of the need to strike an identity. In contrast to Manchester, where we had long since scaled the social heights, in the capital we were expected to prove ourselves all over again. One false move could relegate us for ever to the ranks of the *nouveaux riches*. Of course, we *were nouveaux riches*; the trick was to prove that we could rise above our humble beginnings by living in the style approved by our leaders and creators of high fashion.

We made a start by redesigning our new house as a showcase for Art Deco. The interior of 17 Melbury Road was stripped and cleared to receive bleached wood panelling and clean, light furniture. The sense of space (such a welcome relief from the stuffiness of Lancashire domestic) was enhanced by a liberal use of mirrors. In my bedroom one wall was almost entirely covered by glass, and in the bathroom light was bounced between angular mirrors and black marble tiles. Black and pale white were favourite colours because they emphasized the desire for clean cut choices. The same could be said of those popular emblems of the late 1920s and 1930s the stepped pyramid and the jagged lightning flash – forms which were incorporated into every accessory from a standard lamp to the stair rail. It was all part of the movement towards no-nonsense

48

functionalism. We felt ourselves to be forcing the pace of change.

We employed a full staff, by which I mean a butler, a cook, a scullery-maid, a housemaid, a nurserymaid, a nanny, a lady's-maid, a secretary and a boy who helped out in the kitchen.

The butler, a Jeeves lookalike, was called Ripley, a name which promised dependability. He came with a high recommendation from Flora Solomon whose service he had left when she met hard times. All the servants were in uniform. Ripley had a stiff dark suit and the maids wore blue cotton dresses with caps and aprons. Norman was always referred to as the Master; I was Madam.

Whatever money came our way (and with my stake in Marks and Spencer we were very well off), we spent liberally if not always wisely. We travelled a lot, twice to America in the 1930s, but much more frequently to Paris or the South of France, where the gaming tables added to the spice of life. Weekending in Paris, made possible by courtesy of Imperial Airways, was a great adventure. The flight from Croydon Airport to Le Touquet took about two and a half hours, not much more than we needed to get from Kensington to South London. Some things never change!

Our aircraft was always a Handley Page 42, by modern standards a modestly sized plane which never carried more than forty passengers. We delighted in the little luxuries: a table for refreshments served by two stewards who looked like jockeys (weight was still a major consideration for aviators), electric lights, and hot and cold ventilation. All this was a big advance on flying in the 1920s, when the only service I can recall was a ready supply of cotton wool so that we could plug our ears against the noise of the engines. At that time it was also customary for the pilot to carry a packet of French currency to pay for railway tickets or hotel accommodation in the event of a forced landing. The worst we ever had to face was flight cancellation caused by fog. We then had to scurry off to a supercilious booking agent, who was delighted to tell us that cabins on the cross-Channel sailing were fully occupied. Perhaps, next time, he hinted, we would think more carefully before patronizing the upstart rival.

The natural superiority assumed by everyone associated with boats – even, I suspect, the Woolwich ferry – derived from the enormous prestige enjoyed by the transatlantic liners, the 'floating marvels' of the inter-war years. They were, indeed, the epitome of modern luxury, the trendsetters in comfort and service which other forms of transport could barely hope to imitate. It was no coincidence either that the ocean liner figured so much in contemporary design and architecture. Flat-roofed houses boasted deck terraces, hotel lobbies were made to look like state rooms, and porthole windows appeared everywhere.

It was while we were in New York on our second visit that we discovered the truth about Wallis Simpson. We all knew of her, of course. Who could possibly ignore one of the best-dressed women in society, particularly when she happened to be on close, one might safely guess intimate, terms with the young King? (Tactlessly, perhaps, I had used her dressmaker when, two years earlier, I had been presented at court only to be confronted by a stern-faced Queen Mary.) What was kept from us, by an unholy alliance of politicians and press barons, were the details of her marital experience – one divorce with another about to be finalized – and her intentions for her future happiness to marry Edward VIII and become Queen.

Once in America we were soon brought up to date. Without the restraint of either political discretion or good taste, the gossip columnists were making all they could of the story of a lifetime. Mrs Simpson was as familiar to newspaper readers as Franklin D. Roosevelt, and the resolve of her supporters to make her Queen matched the Democrats' campaign to re-elect the President. Looked at from the American point of view, her chances of success were judged to be high. She came from one of the oldest families – as the press was fond of pointing out, her ancestors had settled in Maryland fifty-two years before the House of Hanover acceded to the British throne.

And since divorce no longer carried a social stigma – how could it in a country which virtually created this profitable legal diversion? – there was nothing to stand in the way of true love. Or so it was argued around the dinner table.

In vain we pointed out that the British establishment was bound to take a less relaxed view of the matter. Even if by some diplomatic sleight of hand the divorce could be settled quietly, there were diehards in power who could not even contemplate an American sharing the crown.It was a horribly snobbish attitude, no doubt, but probably no worse than the inverse snobbery of those of our friends who looked upon Wallis Simpson's ascent to the throne as a decisive victory in the struggle to upstage British society.

It was all very silly. How could we get so excited over such flimsy affairs? But having exhausted The Marriage as a topic of conversation in America, we arrived home to find that the debate was only just getting under way. It was like entering a re-run of a great marathon. The Abdication, though for us totally unexpected, came as an anticlimax.

In the season we spent a week or two in the South of France where, we told ourselves, the sun was brighter.No doubt it was, but since we spent our time mostly at the gaming tables the climate scarcely made any difference. The chief excitement was in watching others play for high stakes. There were always gamblers prepared to risk vast fortunes though, possibly because I had so recently acquired mine, I was never tempted to join them. To compensate for the rare dull moments in the casino, we could bathe, play tennis, go to the theatre, eat good food or simply reflect on how English seaside resorts might profit by adopting the French style of holiday-making. Somehow I could never get worked up by the prospect of a walk on Brighton pier.

The best part of the summer, however, was spent in England in the country. The annual migration was on the scale of army manoeuvres with the hire of a coach and the commandeering of several cars to convey family, staff, animals and numerous items of luggage into rural seclusion. We settled in Kent, though not for any length of time in the same house. We progressed from Sibton Park (now a girls' school) to Plaw Hatch Hall, an early Victorian mansion complete with a nine-hole golf course and a full-time golf pro, to Bassett House, a Lutyens-style building, which we rented jointly with the Sachers.

Bassett House was a great favourite with the children, who were converted the moment they discovered a full-scale model of a pirate ship in the garden. For this delightful incongruity we had to thank Pauline Chase, the actress who had played Peter Pan in the original production. When the show ended its run, she transferred most of the Drury Lane set to what was then her home in the country and left it there when she moved on.

July and August were languid months. Crowds of friends came to stay at weekends, which started early Friday and meandered on until Monday lunchtime. We took our exercise on the tennis court or in the swimming-pool, but the effect of these sporadic bursts of energy must be measured against the hours spent lounging on the terraces gossiping and drinking. As a diversion to the continuing family recital of deals won and lost, we relied on friends from the entertainment business, like the impresario Harry Foster, to add a touch of glamour and risqué excitement. Freddie Brisson was one who always gave good value. Then a publicity expert working for his father, singer and actor Carl Brisson, Freddie was to become a successful Broadway producer and architect of the rise to fame of his actress wife Rosalind Russell.

On the tennis court, I matched my skills against some illustrious players including Danny Prenn, a German Davis Cup champion. Danny, who was one of the first to recognize the appalling threat of Nazism, left his country to settle in Britain just a few weeks after Hitler took power. He came here with just £400, destined as we all thought to become a tennis coach. Instead, he made money by setting up deals for British exporters in the USSR before mounting his own highly successful engineering business. He has always remained one of my dearest friends.

When energy failed, we played contract bridge, a fiendish game then in its early years of popularity. Defeat, always your partner's fault, was an unfailing test of true friendship.

Town and country overlapped on the tennis court and the bridge table. Both games were played enthusiastically, one might say fanatically, wherever we happened to be living. This was the era of tennis and bridge clubs – the natural habitat of the aspiring middle class – though it has to be said that in terms of facilities and players, our family circle precluded any need to join an outside organization.

We each had our own garden tennis court, though Simon's was the finest. Most of the photographs of me in ungainly relationship with a racket were taken at the Marks home in Frognal or at Cleve Lodge, their town mansion close by Hyde Park. In the weeks before Wimbledon, when we were inspired to emulate the heroes of the centre court, invitations to play at Cleve Lodge came so fast that I barely had time to check the identity of my opponents. One game I lost humiliatingly was to an elderly, if athletic, Scandinavian called Gustav. Later he was introduced to me as the King of Sweden.

The great popular entertainments of the inter-war years were the cinema and radio. Yet neither made much impact on my family or friends. For us the entertainment that excelled was the theatre and, in particular, the ballet. We went as much as anything for the spectacle – not only of the productions, though this was the period of grand extravaganzas, but also of the audiences, who were themselves expected to put on a good show. With our sights firmly set on the next issue of the *Tatler*, we put ourselves out to impress, surprise or shock, depending on temperament.

Although by 1930 Diaghilev was gone and his company disbanded, the ballet still held its magic. On any evening there was a choice of entertainments, with the Lyceum, His Majesty's, the Coliseum, Alhambra and the Royal Opera House regularly packing in audiences for their ballet productions. In 1931 the Vic-Wells Opera Ballet made its debut in London. It was the inspiration of two remarkable and determined women: Lilian Baylis, the grande dame of the Old Vic, and Ninette de Valois, the choreographer and former dancer with the Ballet Russe. The reborn British ballet gave us Sadler's Wells, a theatre reconstructed in the style and spirit of the 1930s, where young, magnetic stars like Markova, little Alicia Marks or 'the miniature Pavlova', could stretch their talents.

Even for those with the meanest understanding of dance, the ballet was much more than a theatrical diversion. As the most sensual art form, it was, for both sexes, the trigger for the release of emotions which, in normal circumstances, we could hardly bring ourselves to acknowledge. The hysterical applause, cries of rapture choked by tears, flowers raining down on the stage, the endless curtain calls – yes, it was all a magnificent demonstration of thanks, but was it not also an antidote to a deep frustration within ourselves? Or perhaps just within me?

Spectacle of a more relaxing nature was provided by the musical theatre, notably Drury Lane, where Ivor Novello and Noël Coward ruled triumphantly, and the Coliseum, the English home of the last great operetta. For *White Horse Inn* the entire theatre was transformed into a Tyrolean village in which 160 actors, three orchestras and innumerable yodellers and dancers, not to mention horses, dogs and goats, gave of their best for 651 performances. Some of us went more than once just to see the realistic demonstration of the rain storm at the end of Act Two. It was all clean if damp fun. Sir Oswald Stoll staked £60,000 to mount the show, which allowing for the fall in the pound put it into a higher cost bracket than most contemporary musicals. It may be some encouragement to today's young impresarios to know that Stoll got all his money back, with interest, on advance booking.

After the theatre we had dinner at the Savoy, where you could dance between courses, or, if we really felt daring, we went to a night-club. A feature of all night-clubs, even the most fashionable like the Ham Bone and the Embassy, was their grubbiness. I suppose they had to be dark, dingy and crowded for their customers to believe that they were living dangerously. Certainly, there was not much else to suggest the 'unbridled licence' which puritan critics hoped to find. The West End night life of the 1930s had a veneer of glitter and excitement, but it was empty beneath the surface.

No wonder we all went mad at the Chelsea Arts Ball. The redemption of this overrated event was its rare status as a legal and socially approved opportunity to let off steam. So, as an annual ritual, we got ourselves up in Cossacks' uniforms, a fancy dress which stopped just short of the totally ridiculous, equipped ourselves with a plentiful supply of champagne (because no drink was served at the ball) and gathered at the Albert Hall to welcome in the new year. Then, after five hours of hot, noisy and boisterous revelry, we retreated, picking our way between the bodies towards a welcome gust of morning air. At my last Chelsea Arts Ball, which incidentally, like its predecessor, had little to do with Chelsea and nothing at all to do with the arts, I encountered a bedraggled, sobbing girl who had been soused in what I could only suppose was champagne. I tried to comfort her.

'Never mind,' I said, 'the dress will soon dry out. I'm sure it will be as good as new in the morning.'

She wailed all the louder: 'I don't care about the dress. It was our last bottle.'

From these discursive and fleeting impressions of the 1930s, you will gather that life was a mixed blessing. My little world, with all its material comforts, was self-contained and self-absorbed. Yet, having everything, it promised nothing.

The sensation of time drifting might have been less acute if I had kept up with the social work. But the transition from Manchester to London, and from the modest prosperity to substantial wealth, distanced me from front-line activities. I was on various committees, asked to attend or organize numerous fund-raising dinners, and was always on hand to deputize for Becky in giving little speeches of welcome to guests of WIZO, but it was not what you would call a heavy workload. Hints to Simon that a place might be found for me in the Marks and Spencer hierarchy were dismissed out of hand. If I had been on my own he might have relented, but he was terrified of opening the door to Becky. 'If I let her in,' he once prophesied, 'she'll take over in six months.'

I had no reason to doubt him. An alternative, and one which was urged upon me by contented friends, was to devote more of myself to the family. Though temperamentally unsuited to domesticity, I might have tried harder to adapt if I had felt at all close to Norman. But our slow drift from each other had started even while we were in Manchester. By the mid-1930s we led independent lives. I don't think either of us ever made a conscious decision about our relationship. Living together without emotional commitment was a normal feature of marriage and was sustainable without undue acrimony in a large and well-staffed residence. As he got older, Norman assumed an air of amiable indifference and seemed happiest in his own company, though he was always considerate to the children and took more seriously than I their need for reassurance.

When I felt lonely I turned to the Marks – usually Simon and Miriam – or sought consolation in numbers. I talked about things of no importance with a feigned enthusiasm that suggested freedom of thought but masked all true feelings. If, as the Freudians argued, repression was a social disease, I was in urgent need of treatment.

Something of the sort was said to me by Neville Blond. We met occasionally at Simon's parties when Neville was on one of his trips to London. He had the ability, some might have said the courage, to see straight through my pretensions. He was forthright and ebullient. He always had an idea to occupy him, his own or someone else's. Neville was great fun.

His business was doing well. With his brother Horace, whose wife Rita I had got to know and like when I lived in Didsbury, he had set up Blond Brothers to manufacture raincoats.

'Where could be better than Manchester', he used to say, 'for proving the quality of the product?'

Later, he established a sister company called Fitwell, which supplied Marks and Spencer, among others, with scarves.

What was not going well for Neville was his marriage. This came as a surprise to me as I had assumed that Riva was ideal for him. She was a tall, strikingly attractive woman with an assured sense of her own worth. She was also a match for Neville, who did not appreciate submissiveness, least of all in women.

But Riva had ambitions for them both which Neville was unable or unwilling to fulfil. She hated Manchester and its crude commercialism. At the first opportunity, she moved the family out of the suburbs into rural Cheshire, where she could more easily hold on to the values of gracious living. Neville followed, but reluctantly. Though not without social aspirations, he was most at home in the market place, where he could exercise his talent for shaping events.

If, in some respects, Neville was a disappointment to Riva, so also, it must be said, were her moneyed relatives, Alphonso and Lionel. Though part of the old established Sephardic community, the aristocratic Jews, they, like Neville, were happiest when in the front line of trading. They owned and ran Union Mills, better known to local people as Nahums or, in the Lancashire dialect, Narms. Alphonso and Lionel, who themselves had broad Lancashire accents, couldn't give a toss how their family name was pronounced as long as it was remembered. Riva was more sensitive. Well aware of this, the brothers were none the less unable to resist making fun of her particularly in front of Riva's polite and genteel friends. When Alphonso turned up unexpectedly to find Riva holding a tea party, he burst in at the door, all smiles and simple bonhomie, and enquired loudly, 'Ay up, Riva, how's me bloody country cousins?'

Neville, too, was an inveterate teaser. When Riva declared her support for the family planning movement, the inevitable meetings were held, discreetly of course, to debate policy and to receive advice from the experts. To one of these meetings, Neville addressed an urgent request for help. Introducing himself as a debilitated supporter of five wives and father to seventeen children, he appealed for instruction in the mechanics of birth control as the only way of saving his life. He signed the letter Chief Magumbo. The ladies spent some time discussing how they might tactfully avoid the confrontation.

Riva took this joke in good part, but it was not long before friends began to notice a dangerous overlap between humour and recrimination. When she and Neville were together the anger showed.

Neville spent more of his time away from home. When he was in London he made a point of calling. Conversations at a crowded dinner table led to invitations to an exhibition or a matinee. It was all very discreet and innocent. For more than two years the closest we came to enjoying our own company was at the tea dances at the Savoy. Sanctified by convention and by silly rules – I remember how irritating it was to be told I could not wear the chic French hat I wanted to show off – these tea dances, with their hint of intimacy, held the promise of something more. But of what? The world beyond a slow waltz serenaded by Carol Gibbons's orchestra, with cream cakes to follow, was hard to contemplate. Neville was married with two young sons; I was married with two young daughters. And over us all glowered Simon, the standard bearer of family responsibility and loyalty.

Yet some understanding could surely be expected from my sisters. By now, Becky and Miriam were living what can only be described as open marriages. Both had their affairs; their husbands likewise. Israel, who was Simon's closest friend and business confidant, was a notorious womanizer. With his enormous charm and beguiling cheerfulness, he could be forgiven anything – even, as it happened, an action brought against him by one of the old nobility for alienating the affections of her ladyship. The out-of-court settlement cut a thick slice from the family fortune.

But I could not bring myself even to think of talking about my feelings with anyone except Simon. In the back of my mind there was the sure knowledge that any attempt to bypass him would merely fuel his moral outrage. He expected better things from this youngest sister but, if he was to be disappointed, he had to be the first to know, and the story had to come from me. It was the only chance of a sympathetic hearing. I knew, then, what I had to do. It was simply a matter of choosing the right time, which was not yet.

The Infant Refugees

Neville, meanwhile, remained the sympathetic friend. He gave me confidence, heightened my awareness of what was going on around me and revived my determination to do something constructive.

As a Zionist I did not have to look far for opportunities. Palestine, as ever in the throes of crisis, needed all the help it could get. On the positive side, with the pace of immigration accelerating month by month (much of it clandestine), the Jews in Palestine had emerged as a force to be reckoned with. By 1936 they represented up to a third of the total population. But most of the new arrivals brought nothing with them except their brains and enthusiasm. The peasant farmer from the Ukraine – a typical refugee – needed a piece of land, the equipment to work it and the skills to eke out a living from an inhospitable terrain. All this cost a lot of money, which could only come from the wealthier Jewish communities in Europe and the United States. But however hard we worked, and WIZO with Becky as its driving force achieved miracles, the funds we raised were never equal to the demands on our resources. Palestine was a huge sponge soaking up cash like the desert soaked up water.

Even when we did feel we were getting somewhere – with the opening of a new school or technical college, for instance, or with the successful reclamation of previously arid land – we were aware that it was at the expense of tolerable relations with the Arabs, who looked upon every economic and social advance as an encroachment on their sovereignty. In fact, short of surrendering our right to be in Palestine, it was difficult to know what to do to satisfy the Arabs. In times of prosperity, the Jews were feared; in recession, the Jews were blamed.

Antipathy quickly degenerated into violence. In the late 1920s racial conflict accounted for the loss of over 250 Jewish and Arab lives. The only possible long-term remedy was advocated by the Peel Commission which, in 1937, came out with a recommendation for the partition of Palestine into two independent states. But in none of its dealings was the Chamberlain government attuned to bold and imaginative solutions. Behind a smokescreen of high-flown rhetoric, the Colonial Office held fast to its chosen role as a mediator between the Arabs, who were meant to be reassured by tougher restrictions on immigration into Palestine, and the Jews, who were supposed to take comfort from the British guarantee of their claim to exist in what was still, essentially, an Arab land.

The pressure from our side to allow a more generous quota of refugees into Palestine intensified in direct relation to the deterioration of events in Germany – or, perhaps, it would be more accurate to say in direct relation to our perception of the deterioration of events in Germany. I make this qualification, because there is no doubt in my mind that we – the Jewish community – were slow to register the threat posed by Nazism.

One frequently heard the excuse for inactivity was the fear of reprisals. To create a fuss, went the argument, was simply to aggravate the Germans into making further demands. If Hitler was left alone to work off his temper, he might eventually calm down to a level of rational behaviour.

This was about as fanciful as hoping to tame a mad dog with a kind word and a bar of chocolate. But the tendency to roll over and play dead as a way of deflecting the attentions of an enemy is deep-rooted in animal psychology. It was at the heart of appeasement, the policy which, discredited by history, none the less came closest to expressing the national will. It was not only the Jews who had difficulty in facing reality.

But there were exceptional individuals who understood clearly what was happening and were not prepared to assign the future of German Jewry to the whims of a barbarous demagogue. In March 1933, just a few days after Hitler took power, a party of Jewish notables went to the Home Office to lobby on behalf of German refugees, who were already beginning to appear in this country. The central figure in the delegation was Otto M. Schiff, a City stockbroker whose experience with refugees stretched back to the First World War. It was Schiff who created the Jews Temporary Shelter to give what help he could to immigrants in their first difficult weeks of readjustment. He also set up the Jewish Refugees Committee (later the German Jewish Aid Committee) to ease the way for admission, maintenance, training, employment or re-migration.

Schiff had many friends at the Home Office who trusted his

judgement and respected his humanitarian principles. But he and they both realized that it was useless to expect the British government to adopt an open-door policy to German refugees. The economy was still in deep recession with up to two million unemployed. An influx of penniless refugees could only make matters worse. The counter-argument that Jews, wherever they settled, were more likely to create work for themselves and for others might have been put with greater force but, as we had already discovered in Palestine, or Germany for that matter, success did not necessarily merit approval. It was just as likely to create jealousy and antagonism. Knowing this, Home Office officials warned of a spread of anti-Semitism in this country. With Oswald Mosley and his blackshirts on the march, who was to say their fears were unjustified?

The question remained, what could be done to help the German Jews? Schiff came up with a formula which allowed for a benevolent interpretation of the rules governing immigration. As the law stood, admission could be refused to any immigrant who was unable to show that he could support himself and his family. Very well, said Schiff, we will make that guarantee on behalf of the German refugees and we promise that not a single Jewish refugee allowed into Britain will become a charge on public funds.

The initiative did not lead to any substantial change in the government's restrictive policy on refugees, but it enabled the Home Office to bend the rules in our favour. Notably, the pressure was lifted on those Germans who were here as visitors and who were now unwilling to return.

An appeal launched by the newly created Central British Fund for German Jewry raised an impressive £200,000. Old hands at fund-raising like Becky needed no encouragement to throw their weight behind this latest assault on the middle-class conscience. It was not just sympathy for the underdog; there was the ulterior motive of attracting young people towards Palestine. They saw Britain as some kind of transit camp for their new generation of workers. Sadly, the Foreign Office did not share this rosy vision. Holding fast to the dictum that the number of Jewish refugees allowed into Palestine 'must be strictly conditioned by what the country can absorb', the Foreign Office made clear its opposition to any increase in the quota to allow for German immigrants. But that did not stop them getting in.

By late 1933 the refugee problem was out of the headlines. In the few months when anti-Jewish feeling in Germany was held in check, there was a widespread retreat into wish fulfilment. The fall in the number of refugees arriving in Britain – from 300 to 400 a month at the beginning of the year to less than 100 by the end – was quoted as irrefutable evidence of the capacity for German Jews to come to terms with their new masters. Such was the decline in popular interest that when I accompanied Becky on a fund-raising mission to the north-west, a women's meeting in Blackpool managed to raise an audience of two, one of whom was a local newspaper reporter.

But the lull came to an abrupt end on 13 September 1935. Speaking to the mob at the Nuremberg Rally, Hitler called for new laws 'for the protection of German blood and honour'. For the Jews, these laws amounted to nothing less than a declaration of ostracism. They were to be excluded from the professions, barred from state employment and deprived of the vote. It was not long before Jewish businesses were finding it impossible to operate normally. Bills were unpaid, orders mysteriously cancelled and work sabotaged. Often they were forced to sell out to Aryan competitors at a knock-down price. The plight of German Jews was quickly reflected in the emigration figures, which rose steeply.

Help from the Central British Fund extended from direct cash payments to practical advice on setting up new businesses or starting a new career. It was not easy. Many refugees, who were eminently well qualified to take up important work in this country, came with high expectations which were quickly disappointed. Indeed, the better educated they happened to be, the more likely they were to come up against the restrictive practices of the noble professions. When, years later, I was elected a fellow of the Royal College of Surgeons, I resisted the urge to tell my hosts of my early ill feeling towards that body. It was caused by remarks of the then president, Lord Dawson, who, in 1933, grandly informed the Home Secretary that while there might be room in Britain for a few refugee doctors of special distinction, 'the number that could usefully be absorbed or teach us anything could be counted on the fingers of one hand'. The opposition of the medical establishment to what it described as 'foreign dilution' continued right up to the *Anschluss*. The Home Secretary, Sir Samuel Hoare, left it some years before voicing his disgust: 'I would gladly have admitted the Austrian medical schools en bloc. The help that many of these doctors subsequently gave to our war effort . . . was soon to prove how great was the country's gain from the new diaspora, and how much greater it might have been if professional interests had not restricted its scope.' Quite so.

With the flow of refugees showing no sign of abating, the Central British Fund began to take on the attributes of a permanent organization. Offices were found at Woburn House and Joan Stiebel, recently recruited by Otto Schiff as a private secretary, was quickly slotted in as the administrative lynchpin. She was to stay for nearly fifty years.

More and more, the talk was of long-term solutions with the emphasis on getting out the younger people and helping them to start new lives, ideally in Palestine. Simon was active in drawing up a plan of co-operation with Jewish leaders in the United States. The idea was to raise £3 million in a joint campaign.

But however fast the money came in, it was never quite enough. No sooner did we feel that we were getting to grips with the problems, than another international crisis would throw us into disarray. The Nazi annexation of Austria in March 1938 was the signal for a new wave of anti-Semitism and a huge increase in the applications for refuge in this country. The Central British Fund was all but overwhelmed by paper work, and there were real fears of the money running out. Meanwhile, there were rumours flying about that the Germans were deliberately piling on the pressure to stir up anti-Jewish feeling in Britain. The spectre of thousands of penniless refugees crowding the streets of the big cities was raised by the *Daily Mail* and the *Daily Express*, both of which propagated anti-Semitism in the guise of naive political argument.

Instructions went out from the Foreign Office to its representatives in Europe to tighten up on the allocation of visas and to accept only those who could prove means of support. Since, in Austria, a condition of receiving a passport was a signed undertaking to hand over all property to the state, it was technically impossible for any Jew to meet the conditions set by the British government. Great hopes were pinned on an international conference inspired by President Roosevelt. But the only tangible result of several days' deliberation by the 200 delegates (including thirty-nine Jewish refugee organizations), who gathered at Evian on Lake Geneva, was the setting up of yet another inter-governmental committee. The

British spokesmen took the view that to do anything positive, such as giving open access to refugees, was to encourage the Germans to intensify their efforts to banish the Jewish population.

In October, Schiff told the Home Office that his organization was on the point of collapse. Of the one hundred a day new registrations, up to ninety were destitute Austrians with no hope of employment or of being allowed to emigrate. They lived off whatever scraps of charity could be handed out by the Central British Fund or the German Jewish Aid Committee, the co-ordinating body for all the various organizations involved in the refugee crisis. Hopes of a government grant to relieve the administrative pressure were dashed by a Home Office minister, who declared the 'political impossibility' of financing Jewish immigration. It was a depressing verdict on the character of the government, as indeed on some of the Jewish politicians whose fear of an upsurge of anti-Semitism here overcame their natural sympathies.

The daily scene at the offices of the Central British Fund was heartbreaking. A close-packed queue of human jetsom – the men in baggy raincoats clutching their briefcases, the women in dowdy cotton dresses – stretched far out along the pavement. Inside was a cavernous waiting-room with long benches; there was never a spare seat. As soon as a name was called, everybody moved up a place, eagerly anticipating their own summons to one of the dingy offices. They wanted hope; what they got was, at best, a handout to keep them going for a few more days.

It was with an awful feeling of helplessness that we waited for the next blow to fall. It came in the second week of November. A young Polish Jew, whose parents had been deported from Germany, took his revenge by shooting a senior diplomat. The death of Third Secretary Ernst von Rath from the German embassy in Paris was the signal for a Nazi orgy of violence against the Jews. In the aptly, if chillingly dubbed, *Kristallnacht* (or night of broken glass), shops were plundered, synagogues destroyed, and thousands of innocent people bullied and defiled. There followed a succession of decrees which made it virtually impossible for any German Jew to lead a normal life in his own country. A population of over half a million was deprived of every basic right.

British condemnation of the *Kristallnacht* was unanimous, but the government still restricted itself to 'benevolent interest' in ideas for actually extending a helping hand. One proposal which did gain approval was for simplifying the immigration procedure for children.

The idea came from Norman and Mami Bentwich; he was a law professor with a penchant for humanitarian causes, she a shrewd political campaigner, a former leader of the London County Council. Gathering about them some powerful friends, including Viscount Samuel and Sir Wyndham Deedes, the Bentwichs went to call on the Home Secretary.

In putting their case, Deedes was a powerful advocate. As chairman of the Inter-Aid Committee, he headed an organization which had direct experience of bringing children out of Germany. On the slenderest of resources Inter-Aid had resettled nearly 800 Jewish and Christian children. It was a noble achievement and, as Deedes could testify at first hand, was woefully inadequate.

But of all that party of notables, the true voice of experience belonged to Lola Hahn Warburg. Not that she would have described herself as part of the British establishment. The daughter of a leading Berlin banker, Max Warburg, and sister-in-law of the educationist Kurt Hahn, Lola had lived in this country for barely two months. She and her husband, Wilfred, and two small children were forced out of Germany in September 1938 after Lola discovered that she was on the large blacklist as an outspoken Zionist. Trying to make a home with what little the family managed to bring with them, and still struggling with a language which she delivered with an unmistakable Teutonic intonation, Lola at first resisted Norman's inspired idea to have her join the delegation. But her experience in helping emigrants in the German Jewish community was invaluable, and, in any case, she was too much of an activist to hold out. Along she went as the unofficial but direct representative of mothers and children still trapped in the Third Reich. She was to go on working for refugees throughout the entire war – and beyond.

The response of the Home Office to the Bentwich initiative was encouraging. Sir Samuel Hoare, a well-meaning if second-rank politician, surprised his visitors by hinting at an imminent cut in the red tape to allow in large numbers of refugee children up to the age of eighteen.

Two days later, towards the end of a House of Commons debate on the refugee question, the Home Secretary came out into the open with a clear commitment to dispense with visas and passports for child refugees from Central Europe. All that was needed to gain entry was a single travel document giving a few basic facts issued by a recognized authority. This turned out to be the Movement for the Care of Children from Germany, formed by the Bentwich lobby, which now incorporated Inter-Aid and was soon to become known simply as the Refugee Children's Movement.

Gratitude to the government for what at first appeared to be a selfless act of generosity was soon tempered by the realization of the enormity of the task taken on by part-time and, for the most part, untrained volunteers. Quite apart from the problem of co-operating with refugee groups operating in the viciously hostile environment of Germany and Austria, the RCM was expected to find the money to care for the children for as long as they stayed in Britain. This had the advantage of silencing critics who worried all the time about paying higher taxes to solve other people's problems. But I am not sure the commitment would have been undertaken so lightly if the Jewish community (or the Home Office) had realized that the anticipated re-emigration of the youngsters to Palestine was to prove so difficult. Fearing an upsurge of Arab violence, the Foreign Office all but closed the Palestinian borders. An offer from the Palestinian Jews to adopt 10,000 German children was curtly refused.

By way of recompense, the Foreign Office harried the Colonial Office to come up with alternative areas of settlement – New Guinea was raised as a serious possibility – but good intentions foundered on a mutual apathy: the reluctance of the colonies to add to their cultural and economic problems and the reluctance of the Jews to consider any other home but Palestine.

Meanwhile, the first group of 600 children were on their way from Austria to Holland, where the *De Praag* was waiting at the Hook to bring them on the last leg of the journey across the Channel.

It was at dinner with Simon and Miriam that I first heard about the RCM. I knew of its existence, of course: anyone who read the *Jewish Chronicle* had to be aware of the story. What came as a surprise was the evident lack of planning for such a mammoth enterprise.

'Someone ought to do something,' I protested.

'You're right,' said Simon. 'Why don't *you* do something?'

Knowing most of the people already involved in the RCM, an expression was taken immediately as an offer to exercise my skills as a fund-raiser. This responsibility was eventually translated into the official title of Treasurer. But there was no such thing as job demarcation. Like the other full-time volunteer, Lola Hahn Warburg, I was available for any job that was going, from meeting the latest arrivals at the quayside to checking out prospective foster parents.

In my first weeks with the RCM, I was entirely on my own. Not having an office, I worked mostly from home. Then, in the early days of 1939, a semblance of an organization began to appear. In February the various refugee organizations, representing adults and children, demonstrated a rare capacity for concerted action when they purchased Bloomsbury House, just off Bedford Square, as their joint headquarters. I immediately claimed squatters' rights on a box-like office at the rear of the ground floor.

At the same time the financial strain was eased a little by the success of a radio appeal by Earl Baldwin. In his favourite role as fireside philosopher, the former Prime Minister called for his listeners to come to the aid of victims of a catastrophe, 'not an earthquake, nor flood, nor famine, but an explosion of man's inhumanity to man'. The response added up to a cool half-million, of which £200,000 was allocated to the RCM. Most of this sum went towards maintenance costs, which we put at between £40 to £50 a year per child.

There was cash too from charity premieres and other benefit performances. These events can take up so much in time and administration that they make the box-office returns look very feeble. But by bullying the stars to give their talents and then backing them up with good publicity, we achieved some staggering results. The Broadway singer and comedian, Eddie Cantor, himself the child of Jewish refugee parents, raised £100,000 in a sixteen-day tour of the big cities: Manchester came out on top, I was pleased to see, with a single evening's take of £23,000 – or more than £200,000 at today's values. At Eddie Cantor's wish all the money was put into a special fund to support the re-emigration of young Jewish refugees to Palestine. Bearing in mind the Foreign Office intransigence it might have seemed wishful thinking to devote so much cash to this single cause. But as we got closer to war, we were helped by many a nod and a wink from friends in government to find ways round official obstruction. Within a month of setting up the Eddie Cantor fund, a party of 400 Austrian boys and girls were on their way to Palestine.

Where we failed, despite growing influence in high places, was in persuading the government to open its cheque-book. The question was raised often enough but, always, the overburdened taxpayer was called forth to stand as silent witness against our endeavours. The only pre-war concession was a small tax allowance to families willing to take in refugee children.

Without doubt we would have achieved more if we had lobbied the government earlier and harder. But many prominent Jews were genuinely frightened of stirring up public hostility by seeming to press too hard for special treatment. This was certainly true of Jewish MPs, who, in the long debate on refugees in early 1938, actually took a vow of silence. Their muddled reasoning led them to believe that saying nothing would help to endorse their credentials as model citizens.

In fairness, Jewish inhibitions fell away as closer acquaintance with the ways of government led us to realize what slippery characters we were dealing with. It was unwise to accept any political act at face value. Even the decision to simplify the admission of refugee children was not entirely motivated by selfless generosity. The government acted with one eye on the United States, where public opinion was hostile to British inactivity on behalf of refugees – though less critical of its own government's refusal to relax the immigrant quota.

One of the many unpleasant surprises of 1939 was the failure in Congress of the Wagner-Rogers Bill, which sought the admission to the United States of 20,000 European children. The fear of opening the floodgates prevailed over the more typical American hospitality to refugees.

Thrown back on our own resources, the provision for coping with the influx of bewildered and often frightened children was, to say the least, makeshift. We relied heavily on regional committees, originally set up in Manchester, Birmingham, Bristol and Cambridge, and their local offshoots, to find foster homes and to supervise those children who were put into hostels. They also did their fair share in rallying financial support by encouraging 'workers' circles' to sponsor a number of refugees. A few of these groups even went so far as to buy houses to convert into hostel accommodation. Schools, particularly, felt a close affinity with the young refugees, and offers of free education were worth their weight in gold. Children who spent time in reception camps before moving on to a more homely environment could rely on gifts of food from local tradesmen, not to mention shoes and clothing from the nearest branch of Marks and Spencer.

But the first line of responsibility was at Bloomsbury House. It was there that we had to sort out applications on a first come, first served basis, decide on the number of children the RCM could afford to guarantee (on a government-imposed £50 a head formula) and find guarantors for the rest.

The letters from parents made sad reading: 'This is Heidi, who is twelve; she is lame but very cheerful'; 'Martin is nine, he has a gentle nature and I know you would like him.' But the saddest sight of all was the piles of unanswered, even unopened, letters stacked in the office for weeks after the declaration of war. They stayed there until we knew, absolutely, that nothing could be done.

For children selected by the Jewish refugee organizations in Germany and Austria, we were sent just the essential details with accompanying health certificates. The workers there who sorted out the applications had the agonizing task of facing parents whose children, for one reason or another, had to be refused. I do not know how they did it. But they were magnificent in their dedication and bravery. In saving others, many left it too late to save themselves.

The batches of documents received by the RCM from Kinderauswanderung Abteilung in Berlin and the Kultusgemeinde in Vienna were passed on to the Home Office people who spent all day, every day, issuing permits. The permits went to Passport Control for stamping before coming back to Bloomsbury House, where we returned them by airmail to the Reich. The next hold-up was with the German or Austrian police, who examined each paper with typical thoroughness and, as a matter of callous routine, rejected a proportion as 'incorrect' or, quite simply, 'unacceptable'. The survivors of this bureaucratic obstacle course were given a time and place of departure, often at short notice. Each child was allowed to bring just one suitcase.

A typical Kinderstransport was almost a hundred strong. An RCM representative was nominally in charge of travel arrangements and accompanied the children on the journey, but at the main collecting points, like the central stations at Berlin and Frankfurt, Nazi officials did their worst to keep up the tension.

The farewells were heart-rending. I have been told so many stories – of children not knowing the truth until they were herded together looking back, of parents breaking down in the last moments, of those leaving and those staying racked by fear of the unknown – that I can easily believe I was there.

In reality, my first sight of the young visitors (at this stage we still assumed that they would be moving on to the United States or Palestine before long) was at Harwich or at Liverpool Street. If I was in the RCM party meeting the ferry, I helped in the wearisome business of identification. As a group, the children were immediately recognizable as they filed down the gangplank: they were all neatly dressed as if for a Sunday outing. Girls were distinguished by their wiry pigtails, the boys by their stout boots and sporty belted jackets. Confused and not a little nervous they waited silently in line, like competitors at the start of an obstacle race – which, I suppose, is exactly what they were.

After faces had been matched with the photographs on the travel permits (easier to say than to achieve), each child was securely labelled with name and number. Then, if we had performed our duties efficiently, an immigration official stamped the permits and a medical officer stamped the labels. Only now could we take our charges off the boat for another long wait, this time on the quayside while luggage was searched.

I remember the verdict of a certain man as he went through the suitcase of an eight-year-old girl: 'There's nothing of value here.' He was looking at a doll, a family photograph, a favourite book and a few clothes. It was all she had in the world.

On the train to London we handed out sandwiches. By now the children were more relaxed – or probably just dog-tired, as they had been travelling for the best part of two days. The rhythm of the train and the dusty smell of coal steam was all they needed to send them to sleep.

Those of us in the know were pleased for the respite. The children had to rediscover their energy for the most trying experience of all: the adjustment to a new home and, for some, new parents.

When the train pulled in to Liverpool Street, there was always a line of people waiting on the platform. In front were the guarantors, families who had offered to take in a child and who were eager to catch a first glimpse of their boy or girl. They were inevitably anxious, wondering perhaps, at this critical moment, if they had been too reckless with their hospitality or simply worried about getting over the awkwardness of introductions. One mother told me she was so nervous that when it came to the point she could not remember the name of the boy she was meeting. I am sure that many of the children suffered the same problem in the reverse.

However well meaning, there were guarantors who could behave with dreadful insensitivity – by letting the disappointment show when the flaxen-haired beauty of their dreams turned out to be a tiny tub with pimples, say, or conversely, by building up to such a pitch of enthusiasm for their chosen one that other children in the group felt neglected and inferior. This second group was just as likely to snatch up little Josef or Annette and make for home without telling an organizer. Many an hour was wasted searching the station for a child, presumed lost, but who in fact was already well on the way towards Ruislip. Experience quickly taught us that for the first hour after our arrival, it was the adults more than the children who were likely to misbehave. They had to be watched like hawks.

A small army of RCM volunteers (probably no more than a dozen, but spaced strategically along the platform so that they counted for many more) made room for a reasonably ordered progression from the train to an improvised reception hall – an enclosed space under the taxi ramp at the north end of the station. Seats and benches were set out: on one side, for the children going to foster homes and, on the other, for those destined for hostels and camps. The proper administrative work had to be done, though prospective parents held at bay behind a rope barrier were loath to understand why.

'I don't see why I can't take her now. I'm her auntie, aren't I? Look, here are the papers, Schmitt is the name. I am Mrs Schmitt and Elsa Schmitt is my own husband's brother Max's only child!'

'Yes, yes. I understand. But please, would you mind waiting just a little while!'

Eventually, with everyone talking at once, the RCM lady with the loudest voice had to climb on a chair and appeal for order. A referee's whistle, I found, was a handy aid in these circumstances.

After a few times, the words became routine: 'Will the guarantors please remain behind the barrier until they are called. I will now read the list of names. When you hear your name, please come forward to the table where you can sign the papers and take your child.'

At the end there were always a few guarantors without children (quite possibly they had been taken off the train at the Dutch border; the armed guards liked to give a lasting impression of their authority) and a few children without guarantors. These last joined the bus party waiting to go to one of the RCM hostels.

It was a matter of vigorous dispute within the RCM as to whether foster homes or hostels were the most favoured. There were those like Becky who believed that hostels, with their minimal standard of comfort, were the best training for a hard pioneering life in Palestine. I think she had visions of a strict regime of early morning runs and cold showers. It was not my idea of a proper upbringing, but this was not really the issue. What we had to decide was the likelihood of winning official approval for the scale of emigration Becky had in mind. I had severe doubts and though, in fairness, I must admit that a large number of RCM children did eventually find their way to Palestine, I still feel I was right in advocating foster homes wherever these could be provided. A family life with all its vicissitudes was, in my view, the preparation best suited to every eventuality.

In this meaty dispute, Becky and I found ourselves in some unlikely company. On my side were ranged the timid Jews. They wanted refugees to be dispersed as widely as possible to forestall any anti-Semitic charges of cliquishness. They were backed by a nervous Home Office, who urged that 'in their own interest' children should not be placed together. It was a policy which, taken to its logical conclusion, meant that we might as well give up being Jewish. You can imagine my response. Becky's unwelcome allies were the religious conservatives, who saw the typical middle-of-the-road foster parent as a threat to Jewish orthodoxy. The closed environment of the youth hostel was far better suited to their purposes.

Since neither side was open to persuasion, I and other liberal members of the RCM central committee skirted the religious issue with a reminder that beggars can't be choosers. Even if hostels were thought to be a good thing, there were simply not enough places to accommodate all the children who needed a roof. Help was welcomed from whomever or wherever we could get it, including from Christian families. We were storing up trouble for ourselves, of course. The fanatics would have their day. Meanwhile, my conscience was easier knowing that we were not turning children away on spurious grounds of religious incompatibility.

As the number of young refugees increased, so we were forced to extemporize on accommodation. The offer of free access to two holiday camps – at Dovercourt Bay near Harwich and at Pakefield near Lowestoft – was too good to miss even if, at the best of times, the services were primitive.

Dovercourt Bay was mothered – there is no other word for it – by the formidable Anna Essinger, a gifted teacher who had left Germany in 1933 along with seventy-five of her pupils to start up again in Kent. She was among the first to offer to take in the young refugees. When space was exhausted at her school, Bunce Court, she transferred three teachers, a cook and some of her older pupils to Dovercourt, where together they introduced a semblance of decent living. But Anna was under no illusion about Dovercourt. She thought the place was horrible, and she was right. Built for summer occupation, the chalets and dining hall were, in the hard winter of 1938, like ice houses. The children spent a lot of the time doing exercises, just to keep warm.

It was the same at Pakefield where, in December, we had to organize an evacuation of more than half the occupants: a storm at high tide had brought the sea crashing into their chalets. Two hundred and fifty children were taken to St Felix Girls School in Southwold, where the staff gave up their Christmas holidays to care for them.

With Anna Essinger piling on the pressure, efforts to find foster homes for the holiday camp children were redoubled. Families who showed an interest, usually in response to advertisements or appeals, were invited along to what became known as 'the market', a weekly get-together at which adults and children edged around each other in search of matching personalities. As a technique in applied sociology it lacked subtlety, I know, but even now I would be grateful for any ideas on how we might have done it better. The sadness was always the children who felt unwanted (not, incidentally, the shy and reserved ones who were quite likely to be snapped up quickly by parents looking for an easy option). But the problem of rejection was integral to all our affairs, however well or badly we managed them. In an ideal world we would have checked the characteristics and needs of each of the children and matched them with carefully compiled family profiles. In an ideal world, refugee children would not have existed.

This is not to begin a long-winded justification of all that went into the Movement. We made many mistakes. How could it have been otherwise when most of us had only the experience of our own children to help us along. However, I do like to think I was more worldly than some of my fellow workers. Leading lights such as the Marchioness of Reading, wife of the former Viceroy of India and a stalwart of the Women's Voluntary Service, judged every problem within the narrow conventions of her own class. Refugees were seen as deserving sympathy and help, but they were not to be pampered. This was because, in her view, they were from the lower strata of society. Refugees could not expect, or even appreciate, the finer things in life.

In the context of the RCM she could not have been more wrong. The first groups of children were from well-to-do middle-class families, who recognized the danger they were in and had the knowledge and contacts to do something about it. The children were used to a standard of living higher, on average, than that enjoyed by their foster homes in Britain. Ignoring this fact, Eva Reading would not have believed the story told to me by a bemused parent of his foster child's genuine concern that their shared home did not boast double-glazing. And so, when we needed clothing, it came quite naturally to her to appeal for second-hand articles, for this was how she expected refugees to be dressed. Anything better was an unnecessary indulgence. She even turned down government offers of extra coupons to buy new clothes.

When I heard about this I was furious. No doubt our children had to get accustomed to a simpler and more economical style of life, but it was foolish to ignore an upbringing which had taught them to regard everything second-hand as second-rate – a badge of humiliation. I tried to counterbalance Eva Reading's misplaced efforts by appealing to some of my relatives in California to organize a collection – I even sent the measurements of our neediest clients. The response was magnificent. More to the point, it was beyond Eva Reading's power to divert the resources to her own pet schemes.

Before going any further I must make clear that the RCM was not alone in helping children escape Nazi persecution. With all the courage of latter-day Pimpernels, kind people like Trevor Chadwick, a prep school teacher, and Jean Hoare, a cousin of Sir Samuel Hoare, took flights to Prague where they organized their own transport. It was here that their endeavours were best appreciated for there was no central Jewish organization in Czechoslovakia – just a small group of English volunteers willing to brave the Gestapo bureaucracy. Both Trevor Chadwick and Jean Hoare were members of the Society of Friends, the body which did most to help young refugees. In any appeal for aid, the Quakers were among the first to open their homes and their pocket-books.

Also separate from the RCM but very much part of the Jewish community was the Chief Rabbi's Religious Emergency Council (CRREC), which, as its name implies, was preoccupied with preserving the faith in all its formal panoply. Overlorded by Rabbi Solomon Schonfeld and Harry Goodman, the CRREC operated two hostels – d'Avigdor House in Bedford Row for boys and Worthfield in Stamford Hill for girls. Admission was strictly limited to refugee children from orthodox Jewish families, which was fine until the Rabbi decided that the RCM should subscribe to their narrow view of life. They gave us more trouble and occupied more precious time with pettifogging complaints than all our other critics put together.

Happier relations were kept with another orthodox group, Youth Aliyah, a German-based organization which prepared young Jews of all denominations for emigration to Palestine. Persecution at home initiated a London office as half-way house. But with the difficulty of getting permits to move on to Palestine, the Youth Aliyah representatives here were soon concentrating on getting children out of Germany without worrying too much about the next stage in their journey. Accordingly, about 500 Youth Aliyah refugees, arriving mostly by RCM transport, were posted to rural settlements (*Hachshara*). There, inspired by Zionist values and warnings of the hard life to come in Palestine, they embarked on a vigorous training in subsistence farming. Offers of foster homes were rejected out of hand. The children had to be kept together in their social and religious enclaves.

While not approving wholeheartedly of Youth Aliyah's priorities, I supported the RCM decision to help financially. Dedication

74

deserved reward. But, as time went on, I cannot say I was surprised by reports of a deterioration of the missionary spirit. With the journey to Palestine postponed indefinitely, some refugees began to assume that they would never get there. Others wondered if they really wanted to go. As doubts set in, the cause was lost. No doubt those Youth Aliyah boys and girls who were eventually assimilated into British society kept their Jewish identity. But for this, I continue to believe, they were called upon to sacrifice too many family comforts.

The last pre-war transport arrived at Harwich in the late morning of Friday, 1 September 1939. It was a close-run thing. The day before we had heard that the Dutch-German border was closed and that there was no point in the children leaving Berlin. But someone at the Youth Aliyah office refused to take no for an answer. A frantic session of telephoning evoked a promise from the Dutch to wave through the young refugees on the assurance that Britain too would allow freedom of entry. The commitment was given and word sent to Berlin, where the children were put on a train to Kleve, a small border town not far from Nijmegen. A bus was waiting for them. There followed a roundabout journey with the driver stopping frequently to ask directions. When they heard who was on board, villagers turned out to cheer the youngsters on their way.

We expected sixty-six arrivals. In the event, the Germans set an arbitrary limit of sixty, so the youngest were left behind. In the weeks following we made a tally of the records at Bloomsbury House. We had welcomed 9,354 refugee children, of whom about eighty per cent were Jewish. Taking into account the children brought in by groups like Youth Aliyah, the total was well over the 10,000 (another arbitrary figure) originally anticipated by the Home Office. Up to the end of 1939, only 330 of our children had re-emigrated. A further 1,150 departed by late 1942, after which movement out of the country virtually ceased until after the war.

But movement in did continue, if only at a trickle. On 14 May, four days after the German invasion of the Netherlands, forty German and Austrian children from an Amsterdam orphanage were driven to the port of Ijmuiden. The organizer of the escape, Gertrivida Wijsmuller-Meijer, put them on board a small cargo vessel, the *Bodegraven*, which sailed for Britain late that evening. The story nearly ended tragically. Emerging out of the early morning mist off Cornwall, the boat was spotted by a local defence unit who promptly assumed the worst. But at the sound of gunfire the *Bodegraven* turned smartly away and made off up the coast, where it was eventually permitted to dock at Liverpool. Immigration formalities were waived and the children were taken in by the Manchester branch of the RCM, where Riva Blond was the driving force.

By the outbreak of war, the RCM was in reasonable administrative shape, given our limited resources. We had a hard-working and dedicated general secretary, who was full time at Bloomsbury House and on salary – albeit a pittance. Dorothy Hardisty was like a good head teacher, firm but kind. She had a prodigious memory for names and faces, a quality which gave her a head start on her predecessor, Sir Charles Stead, a retired Indian civil servant who quickly and mercifully recognized that the job was too much for him. Our chairman was Lord Gorell, who achieved fame in the First World War as the founder of the Royal Army Education Corps. Though we saw him rarely at Bloomsbury House, he had a critical role to play in our relations with Whitehall. He also gave valuable service as an independent arbitrator in the internecine battles soon to break out over religious education. I asked him once if he knew at the beginning what he was letting himself in for. He told me no, but added that he had not been quite so naive as to believe an assurance from the Archbishop of Canterbury that his 'duties would not be very exacting'.

Much of the day-to-day work of keeping contact with the children in their foster homes fell to the local committees, of which there were eventually 175. In some areas we separated Jewish and Christian helpers, but mostly they favoured a joint organization. It was the same at regional level, where we adopted the boundaries set for the twelve defence areas. There was much to-ing and fro-ing between the central organization and its branches. Hostel inspection was necessary, of course, shared by Dorothy Hardisty, Lola and myself, but visits to individual foster homes took up a lot of travelling.

Looking back on the records, we spent what must now seem an unnecessary amount of time on the minutiae of domestic accounting.

'Erich needs a suit very badly. He is growing up fast.' Erich's wish was granted.

'Ruth needs two pairs knickers and one apron.' Ruth was awarded her knickers but not the apron. 'An unwarranted expense,' declared her supervisor, though what the poor girl was supposed to do to stop herself getting mucky in the kitchen, I cannot imagine.

'Hans is returning to London. He has no suitcase.' Nor did he get one, at least not from the Movement, but he did get some free advice: 'Borrow one.'

Mean? No, not really. We relied for our income on private donations for which there were now many competing claims, not least on behalf of the thousands of adult refugees protected by the Central British Fund. Time and again we went back to the Jewish community to bail us out. We never came away empty-handed, but it did not take a crystal ball to forecast disaster within months unless the government came to our aid.

One of the Family

We heard the good news in October 1941. From then on the Home Office was to pay maintenance of up to nineteen shillings a week for every child – just enough for subsistence. Moreover, the RCM was to receive a grant amounting to seventy five per cent of administrative costs. We began to feel a little less as if we were under siege. We were not rich, far from it, but we could survive.

What of the children themselves? Within a year the younger ones were drinking tea and eating Yorkshire pudding without turning green. English had taken over from German as the first language and names were Anglicized. But it was easy to teach new tricks; easier still to assume that adapting to practicalities was proof of balanced personalities. It could not be so. For many, the emotional wounds were too deep for rapid healing. They had seen their parents ill-treated and humiliated, they knew about the camps and Hitler's final solution. Sometimes, more out of kindness than any malicious intent, foster parents or relatives prepared them to hear the worst; sometimes they could not take it.

Moritz, a Polish boy born in Cologne, was a smiling, good-looking child when he arrived in June 1939. Aged thirteen, he spent two years at a Cardiff school, where he learned English, and then trained as an electrician. About the time he started work he became obsessed that he would never see his parents again; he feared that they were already dead. He was probably right. Authority, any authority, was blamed for the tragedy. Moritz antagonized his employer, who promptly sacked him, and refused help from his friends. In 1942 he was persuaded to go into hospital, where he was said to be schizophrenic. A year later he was certified insane. His letters spoke of torture, of being forced to sit alone all day, forbidden to move from his chair. It was not like that; well, not quite. Because no one had any idea of how to treat his illness, Moritz was kept in isolation for his own and for other patients' safety.

An entry towards the end of his record card describes Moritz as 'looking very thin and pale'. His visitor tried to talk with him, but 'discussion is difficult as he keeps repeating whatever I say'. In April 1946 we were told that Moritz was critically ill. Tuberculosis was diagnosed, and he died in September. You might say that he committed suicide in stages.

Norbert was another boy who took to himself the agony of persecution suffered by his parents. Often in trouble with the police who stood in for the real enemy, he was unable to keep a job for more than a few weeks. We last heard of him in August 1950, when he came of age. 'Norbert reports regularly to the Labour Exchange,' someone wrote, 'but has no intention of working. He is not easy at the hostel and it is possible that he will have to return to hospital, but at the moment, he is not certifiable.'

There were, thank God, many happier stories. They are recalled now by brief notes scribbled in haste. (It was always the problem children who had the longer reports.) I think I can put a face to Edward, a weekly boarder at Rowan House School where he was described as a 'brilliant pupil'. At the end of the war Edward was reunited with his mother and returned with her to Germany to become a highly successful engineer.

And there was Eva, said to be 'weak and difficult to deal with' when she arrived, but who got to Oldham Grammar School. She lived in one room with an aunt who worked night shifts. Eva decided early on that she wanted to be a teacher. When, entirely by her own efforts, she was accepted by a training college, the RCM helped out with a grant. Later, she went on to study full time at London University.

The luckiest ones, it might be thought, were those who rediscovered their parents. But reunion, either during or after the war, was not always a happy experience. Adapting more readily to a new culture, children could be brutal to their elders who found it difficult to rise above the status of humble, charity-seeking refugees. After three or four years apart, there could even be a crisis of simple communication, the parents not having learned English and the children having forgotten their German.

Setting down her impressions soon after the end of the war, Dorothy Hardisty recorded the bewilderment of parents who were treated like strangers by their own children. 'It was our saddest time', she wrote, 'when children "went home" to be miserably unhappy.'

For most, of course, these problems did not arise. They never saw their real parents again. The more fortunate found new families here, foster parents who gave them love and respect.

How easy it is to take their generosity of spirit for granted. In reality, the task of the foster parent, however capable and well meaning, was hard and, in the early relationship, often thankless.

Children who had run the Nazi gauntlet were naturally suspicious of authority. They could easily fall into depression, and who can blame them? They showed fear or anger in circumstances which had to be explained to unknowing adults (as, for example, when refugee children were told to put on brown shirts as part of their school uniform) and they were quick to assume hostility. What for an English child was a harmless joke (say, an imitation of a German accent) could, for a refugee child, swell into a mortal insult.

There were problem foster parents too. Outraged by an accusation of hostility or cruelty, they none the less treated their refugee children as second-class citizens: at best unpaid servants, who had to prove their gratitude by fawning subservience; at worst social misfits, who were likely to embarrass their elders in front of the neighbours. I am ashamed to say that nearly all these awkward customers were Jewish.

The necessities of war added to the pressures. No sooner were the later arrivals settled in with their foster parents than they were up and off again in the national evacuation from the big cities, the first targets for German bombs, to the countryside. When the expected Blitzkrieg did not happen, many of the refugee children returned to their first English homes; others were reconciled to rural seclusion. The country life was favoured by the strongly Zionist element in the RCM who still visualized an eventual exodus of eager young farmers to Palestine, and by the government who wanted to recruit labour to the hard-pressed agricultural industry.

It was a coincidence of interests which Becky spotted even before the war when, much to everyone's surprise, she got official backing for recruiting over 1,000 apprentice farm workers from Germany and Austria. They were to continue training and put in a decent spell of work on British farms in return for jumping a few places in the queue for visas to enter Palestine. Becky was in the front line of the Jewish Agricultural Committee which, in co-operation with Youth Aliyah, ran sixteen training centres. To all her young followers, she promised a healthy and invigorating life.

At Bloomsbury House we had to recognize that farming was not a universal passion. Depending on age, our children worked their way through the educational or vocational training system like any of their English contemporaries. But then, they were not quite like the others, because there was no official encouragement for them to aspire to higher education or a career in the learned professions. What today is designated as the closed shop was operated against talented young people who just happened to be refugees. It was inspiring to find how few of them were put off. Already used to the hard slog, they persevered at evening classes and with correspondence courses to achieve the qualifications denied to them in open competition.

I suppose that some prejudice against older teenagers of German or Austrian origin was inevitable. At the beginning of the war when public morale was low and rumours of imminent invasion abounded, anybody who was obviously alien was liable to be identified as a fifth columnist. As one crushing blow followed another – the collapse of Holland, the surrender of Belgium, Dunkirk, the fall of France – the suspicion of foreigners mounted to hysteria.

Lola Hahn Warburg, with her pronounced German accent, often found herself in trouble. On a tour of inspection in North Wales, an innocent request for directions attracted a police escort which followed her, at a safe distance, for several miles.

One of our girls was reported for sketching a village green (an unlikely military target), and a boy who was overheard describing his home in Vienna was branded as a spy, though presumably not a very intelligent one.

In fact, there was a close check on those youngsters who were over sixteen. All of them had to register with the police and those from Germany and Austria had to persuade a tribunal of worthies that they were not a threat to security. The great majority were eventually put into Category C under the incongruous heading 'Friendly Enemy Alien' or, more reasonably 'a refugee from Nazi oppression'. In the agonizing wait for this welcome verdict, a period of several weeks, the youngsters were automatically designated Category B. This meant that they could not travel freely about the country – no great inconvenience in itself – but it also implied they were liable to act against the national interest, a slur the RCM resented. Sadly, our protests to the Home Office got us nowhere until the threat of immediate invasion was lifted. By then, a change in the rules was too late to save the RCM boys who were rounded up under the internment orders of May 1940. One of the first decisions of the Churchill government, the order of 10 May, was part of a plan to tighten security along the vulnerable south and east coasts. All male Category B Germans and Austrians who happened to be living in these areas were detained, among them boys just past the age of sixteen who were taken from foster parents or schools without explanation. A country-wide internment order issued a week later affected all male Category B aliens aged between sixteen and sixty.

About 1,000 RCM boys were involved. They were sent to hastily constructed camps, the biggest of which were at Huyton, near Liverpool, and on the Isle of Man. Life there was miserable. Young and old were thrown together, sharing rooms and beds. A Jewish adolescent who had every reason to hate Nazism could find in his closest companion a devotee of fascism who counted Hitler among the saints. And nobody knew what was going on.

Our complaints, though vigorous, were not at first taken seriously. I was not the only one at the RCM to be told by a Home Office official that refugees wanted to be interned; how else could they be protected from the angry natives who blamed them for causing the war? Making the best of a bad job, we sent in books, recruited volunteer teachers (there were internees preparing for their school certificates) and explained to the supervisors the intricacies of the kosher diet. One group of Youth Aliyah boys were allowed to grow and prepare their own food, a form of self-help which did something to alleviate the tedium.

But as ever in our business, no sooner had we come to grips with circumstances than another crisis intervened. In June 1940 we were summarily informed that internees were to be shipped off to the Dominions – indeed, that the *Duchess of York* with 2,600 passengers, including a handful of RCM teenagers from Huyton, was already on its way to Canada. Close behind was the *Arandora Star*, which sailed from Liverpool on 1 July. Her voyage was ended prematurely off the west coast of Ireland by a German torpedo: over 600 passengers and crew were lost. Such was the official secrecy – or confusion – that it took several weeks to discover that none of our boys were among the casualties.

Three other sailings which left shortly after the *Arandora Star* did include teenage refugees from the RCM and Youth Aliyah. As far as we could gather, the unlucky ones were picked at random, though a few had asked to go with their friends. Their treatment was shameful. On the *Ettrick* bound for Canada and the *Dunera* sailing for Australia, crew and military escort behaved so abominably as to prompt questions in the House of Commons and demands for a full-scale enquiry.

Yes, it was war; yes, there were other pressing matters to occupy the government; yes, we agreed there were times when the welfare of individuals had to be subordinated to the interests of the state. But, no, we could not excuse the intrusion of the Nazi mentality into the management of our affairs.

A passenger on the *Ettrick* recorded these memories soon after he landed:

We were herded together in the bows of the ship in a three-tiered space with a shaft in the centre. The three tiers were connected by companion ways – the top tier was at about sea level. Most of the space was taken up by dining tables, benches, the shaft and the companion ways. At the top level, over 500 people lived and slept for twelve days and nights.

In the event of an emergency the only way out for the internees on the lower tiers would have been the companion way and from there to the lower deck, but at the top of the companion way there was a barbed-wire barrier which left a space of some 4ft for passage during the day, but was entirely closed and under military guard during the night. To reach the upper deck and the lifeboats we would have had to get through another barbed-wire barrier and two further companion ways, which were always heavily guarded, while the doors at the top of the companion ways were kept locked.

The only supply of air came through the ventilating pipes which ran through the body of the ship.

Not enough hammocks and blankets were issued to the internees, people slept on the dining tables, on the benches, on the floor, on the companion way, literally on top of each other.

For two days we were not allowed to emerge, for we were not to see any part of the Scottish or Irish coast. After that, congestion was relieved during the daytime by two-hourly shifts of half the complement on deck. There were two inadequate meals a day, one at 8 a.m. and one at 6 p.m.

Many people were sea-sick almost the whole time, and a few buckets were allotted to them, and put down among the people who had to lie on the floor at night. During the second night a sudden epidemic of diarrhoea broke out. The gangway leading to the lavatories was closed by barbed wire, and as the guards refused to open them even in an emergency, people had to relieve themselves wherever they stood or happened to be. This situation was repeated during the following night, and the prisoners were finally granted another few buckets, for which there was hardly any room left on the floors where people were lying.

After their arrival in the Canadian camp all the refugees' belongings were taken away by NCOs and privates. They were told that everything would be returned the next morning. However, when two days later the luggage and confiscated goods were returned it was discovered that money and such things as watches, pens, lighters had disappeared. While the luggage was laid out for examination and collection, the thieving continued.

Conditions on the *Dunera* were even worse: 2,400 Jewish refugees and prisoners of war were transported in a ship built to carry only half their number. They were robbed, bullied and humiliated. From the catalogue of horror stories about the *Dunera*, the victims were least likely to forget the guards' favourite sport of scattering broken glass across the deck just before giving the order to exercise – in bare feet.

Four hundred RCM boys were deported, but there it stopped. The outrage of press and Parliament, hitherto leaders of the campaign to deport all foreigners, led to the cancellation of further transports and to a popular demand for the release of Jewish internees in this country. Among the first to be freed were the under-eighteens who had foster parents to go to. Within a year most of those who had been sent abroad were allowed home.

Was it any comfort for those who unjustly suffered deportation to know that they helped their adopted country to rediscover its conscience and to remember why exactly it was fighting a war? I hope so because they performed a great service.

Our children grew up. Why we should have been surprised, I cannot imagine, but what with one thing and another we were not wholly prepared for the transformation of tame infants into rebellious adolescents. The first rule was to be firm. Unfortunately, not all of us could be relied upon to obey it. Of the central committee, Leonard Montefiore, who was also the treasurer of the Central British Fund, was the first to accede to demands, usually for more pocket money. What he failed to see was that in satisfying one complaint, he started a succession of others. Or perhaps he did not worry too much. I fancy he rather enjoyed his reputation as a soft touch.

Lola and I were the toughies. Those on the receiving end who recall those days are kind enough to say we were also fair. I hope they are right. Anyway, we tried. However, there were occasions when we almost lost control of events. I turned up one morning at Bloomsbury House to find Lola sharing her office with a party of angry young men.

'It's a deputation,' she explained. 'They want me to reinstate Ashby.'

Ashby was a man of dubious reputation who somehow managed to get himself appointed as the warden of one of our hostels. Lola had recommended and pushed through his dismissal. Evidently, he could still rally support.

'Is there anything I can do?' I asked.

'What do you suggest?'

Offhand, I could not think of a constructive proposal.

The occupation lasted for most of the day. Lola persuaded her visitors to elect two spokesmen with whom she talked while the others waited in the corridor. But however hard-pressed, we refused to say why the warden had been sacked. It was unfair on the man, she argued, to make the details of the case public. Throughout Bloomsbury House there was only one topic of conversation – who would crack first? In the end the prize for endurance went to Lola, who made it clear that she was prepared to spend the night in her office if it was necessary to win her case. For the boys, hunger pangs dictated the wisdom of an honourable withdrawal. They asked for fourteen shillings each for the train fare home. Lola said that she could not possibly justify the expense, but they knew and she knew that Leonard Montefiore would pay. There were no hard feelings. When Lola visited the hostel a few weeks later, the boys presented her with a large bunch of lilacs.

Another sort of rebellion – altogether more virulent – came from within our own members at Bloomsbury House. I mentioned earlier the religious issue and the conviction of the CRREC that we were not doing enough to protect the Jewish faith and tradition. It was a charge I rejected out of hand. The evidence of religious laxity was based on our failure to achieve a perfect match between Jewish refugees and Jewish foster homes. It is true that up to a third of our children were placed with Christian families, but it was a simple fact that more non-Jewish than Jewish homes were offered. This was hardly surprising given that the Jewish community represented barely one per cent of the total population.

We did make a special effort to place orthodox children with sympathetic adults willing to follow strict dietary rules and to make allowances for other religious observances. But even here we could not guarantee success. Offers of orthodox homes dried up as early as April 1939. What were we then supposed to do? Turn children away and tell them to make the best of it in Berlin?

In fact, what we did was to accept as many children as we could get in – orthodox, liberal and non-believing – on the assumption that all other problems were secondary and could be tackled, one way or another, as we went along.

In the early days few of our children were allowed to forget their Jewish connections. Those who went to live with Christian families were invited to Jewish households for festivals and fasts, Jewish teachers were encouraged to set up special classes and kosher canteens were opened. There was even a correspondence course for the Barmitzvah. But as our numbers swelled, attention was distracted from the details of religious formalities. Left to their own devices children were, quite naturally, inclined to veer away from any outward show of orthodoxy. They wanted to be like the others – and the others, more often than not, were middle-of-the-road Church of England.

Our efforts to protect Judaism were dealt another blow by the evacuation which took children out of the cities – the centres of Jewish influence – and put them down in the countryside, where

Elaine as a child with her brother
Simon Marks.

Elaine aged three.

At the wedding of her sister Rebecca to Israel Sieff, 1910, Elaine sits in the centre of the
front row; her brother Simon, the best man, stands behind to the right of the bride.

Elaine and Norman Laski's wedding day, 1926. The best man was Neville Blond; the page and bridesmaid, Michael and Hannah Marks.

Elaine, soon after arriving in London.

About to be presented at
Court, early 1930s.

In fancy dress, 1930s.

With Ann and Simone just before setting off to America, 1948.

With Becky (centre) and Prime Minister David Ben-Gurion in the early days of the
State of Israel.

Gotwick Manor, East Grinstead, the home Elaine shared with her second husband, Neville Blond (below).

The Queen Mother talks to the Bishop of Guildford during the ceremony to lay the foundation-stone of the Burns Unit, 1963. Neville (centre) and Elaine are on the platform with her.

With an Arab Druze family at Tel Mond, Israel, January 1966.

With Simone (left) and Ann, standing in front of a portrait of her father, Michael Marks, 1968.

Opening the Elaine &
Neville Blond Crèche
in Israel, 1974.

Making a presentation to Prince Philip at a Guinea Pigs reunion, early 1970s.
Lady McIndoe is in the centre.

Cutting her eightieth birthday cake, with Marcus Sieff (left) looking on.

With her son-in-law David Susman a few weeks before her death, 1985.
Michael Sacher is in the background.

Christian values were not lightly disregarded. On our journeys out of London – braving the blackout and, that most irritating of wartime restrictions, the absence of signposts – we encountered genuine acts of kindness to the young visitors which could, none the less, be embarrassingly inappropriate. Here was a rural vicar who went out of his way to make two Jewish sopranos feel at home by recruiting them to his church choir; there, a farmer's wife who persuaded her husband to kill the fatted pig so that the family and their Jewish guests could enjoy a slap-up roast.

Acknowledging our sins of omission, in 1941 we made a direct appeal to Jewish organizations to support religious education. The result was not quite what we anticipated. A plethora of high-sounding pressure groups, divided under orthodox and liberal banners, promptly took up cudgels against each other. The RCM held the middle ground though, naturally, because we had a liberal majority, we were said to favour their interests. This was certainly the view of the CRREC and its offshoot, the Union of Orthodox Hebrew Congregations (*Adath*). In the full torrent of impassioned debate Rabbis Schonfeld and Goodman could make us sound like undercover agents for the Archbishop of Canterbury.

The religious issue came to a head in 1944. That year the bill was put through Parliament allowing for the appointment of a legal guardian for our unattached children – about 4,000 in all. The religious significance of the change did not at first occur to us. All we wanted to do was to escape from the administrative straitjacket whereby guardianship could only be granted on the basis of individual applications. Hitherto the RCM was merely 'in loco parentis', which meant, for example, that we were strictly limited in our power to remove a child from an unsuitable foster home. There were problems too with the hospitals where, technically, an operation could not be performed on a child unless consent was given by a parent or guardian. I discovered this at first hand when I arranged for a fourteen-year-old girl to have surgery on her club foot. Fortunately, I dealt with an enlightened no-nonsense medic. 'If I had to wait for the proper signatures,' he boomed, 'I'd never get anything done.'

There was really only one candidate for the role of guardian – our chairman, Lord Gorell. As he himself admitted, given his position of seniority within the children's refugee movement, it was unthinkable that the Home Secretary should look elsewhere. But his otherwise excellent qualifications were marred by a single detail: he was a Christian. For the watchdogs of orthodoxy, if not for the rest of us, this was a matter of great concern. Their criticism was linked to that part of the Guardian Act which opened the way for our orphan children to become naturalized British subjects; from then on it was a single formality for them to be adopted by their foster parents. Fine, so far. But what if the foster parents were Christians? Lord Gorell might support their beliefs in defiance of Jewish claims.

In my frequent and fiery discussions on the subject, I argued that you did not have to be a Christian to recognize the justice and simple humanity of preserving the relationship between foster parents and the children they loved. The alternative – seriously advanced – of transferring all Jewish children in Gentile homes to a suitably orthodox environment, would hurt everyone involved and was, in any case, impracticable.

In early 1944, Harry Goodman and Solomon Schonfeld together with other leading lights of *Adath* came out into the open with the publication of a vitriolic attack on the RCM. Renamed 'The Child Estranging Movement', we were berated for our failure to keep to the narrow path of spiritual purity. I will not dwell on the tedium of the ensuing debates; I need only say that the records – still thankfully in existence, if in a somewhat chaotic state – will confirm that the RCM did all in its power to hold to the principle of raising children in the religion of their parents.

There were numerous cases where young people lost interest in formal religion (a sequel of war which touched every faith), several cases of intermarriage and a few cases where Jews converted to Christianity. These last, held by our opponents to demonstrate a deeper malaise, were the object of intense enquiry; almost, one might say, an inquisition. The rows saw out the life of the RCM. As late as 1948 we were considering a request from a fifteen-year-old girl who wanted to become a Catholic. By way of a compromise, I suggested that she should spend a few months in a Jewish home. This was agreed, but the experience did not alter her convictions.

The following extracts from two letters give a fair indication of the bitterness of such disputes. On 13 January Dayan Swift wrote to Lord Gorell:

Your decision in the case of Susanne Karpathi – i.e. to consent to the handing over of a young Jewish orphan of fifteen years of age to another Faith in spite of the report of the Rev. Fabricant and the sworn statement of Mr Uszer Blumstein – has completely shaken my confidence in you as Guardian of our Jewish children. In the circumstances I must ask you to accept this letter as an intimation of my resignation from the Movement unless, of course, I hear from you that you are prepared to withdraw your consent to the baptism of this child. In the event of not hearing from you within the course of a week, I shall take it that you accept my resignation. It will then be necessary for me to make a statement in the press and present a report on this case to the religious and lay leaders of the Jewish community.

To which Lord Gorell replied:

I am naturally sorry that you should be resigning from the Executive of the Movement, though I felt that your breach of confidence in respect of Bishop Craven's letter and your subsequent discourtesy, indeed hostility, to him at our last Executive made that almost inevitable. I had hoped that, in spite of occasional differences of view – astonishingly few when all these years and all the thousands of children are considered – we should have all been enabled to continue to work together to the end. But that, clearly, is not to be. Of course, I cannot change my decision because you will resign if I do not. I gave it, quite impartially, as the decision in the best interests of my ward, after a most careful study of all the facts and after a long personal talk with that ward. I accept your resignation accordingly.

I am puzzled and pained, I must say, at the lack of appreciation you show, and have long shown, for the work of the Movement. I do not remember your ever saying a word in acknowledgement of the unstinted care and loving kindness which, for years on end, Christian foster parents have, in hundreds of cases, lavished utterly disinterestedly upon Jewish refugee children. Always you have shown suspicion and even rancour, and now in this case – the very first of its kind I have had to deal with in all the nine years of my Chairmanship – the moment I am compelled by the facts to differ from you, you tell me your confidence in me is 'completely shaken'. Very well; so be it. I accept that also, grieved though it makes me.

As for the formal declaration, dated December 24th, 1947, from Mr Blumstein, I can only say that, as far as I am aware (and I have gone very deeply into the case), he has never in all the years of Susanne's life in this country made any attempt at all to see or help her or taken any interest in her whatsoever. Moreover his declaration is decidedly contrary to the evidence in several essential particulars.

I note that you intend 'to make a statement in the press and to present a report to the religious and lay leaders of the Jewish community'. I must therefore ask that it be a complete one including this letter.

To make my own position clear, I too wrote to Lord Gorell:

I can assure you that there has never been any lack of confidence in you as either Chairman or Guardian. On the contrary, I could not have wished to have served under a more painstaking or fair-minded person. I would like to say how much I disapprove of anything that may have been said to the contrary.

And that was that.

With the ending of the war, I expected the work of the RCM to wind down quite quickly. Our youngsters were beginning to make their own way in the world. Those with parents still officially listed as missing had long since given up hoping for a miracle. We filled in the search forms (names, last seen and so on), fed them into the system and waited for the invariable response: died in a concentration camp. It was difficult to relate the humdrum routine of the filing clerk to the horror stories coming out of Germany as, one by one, the camps were exposed. But then, unexpectedly, we were pushed back into the front line. A request came through to take on the rehabilitation of children who had miraculously survived the camps. It appeared that we still had a job to do.

The instigator of the scheme for the Care of Children from Refugee Camps (yet another committee!) was Leonard Montefiore. He was in

Paris in May 1945 when they began the airlift of survivors direct from the camps. He told me later: 'I have never seen anything so ghastly in my life. The people I saw were like corpses who walked.' What of the children? They were among the early arrivals, but Leonard assumed that there were young survivors still to be found. Within the month he had obtained Home Office approval for bringing into Britain up to 1,000 camp orphans. A note of unreality was introduced by the civil servants who required that all the children should be under sixteen. Since the chances of finding anyone who had documentary evidence to prove their age were unlikely, Leonard persuaded Whitehall to accept his guesswork. It was a responsibility which he interpreted liberally.

The next step was to create the semblance of an organization, a task to which I now diverted my energies. Meanwhile, an approach was made to the army, who told us that we were wasting our time because no children had been found. We kept hoping. In July we heard about a group who had been saved from the Theresienstadt camp in Czechoslovakia. There were about 300 who were fit to travel. A reception centre on Lake Windermere was made ready for them.

I am not quite sure what we expected; a collection of skeletons, I suppose, smaller versions of the tragic figures we had seen on film staring through their skulls at the cameras of their liberators. They were not like that. There were a few invalids, but the rest looked reasonably fit and strong. Of course, they had to be to have got so far. But the outward appearance of toughness did not mean that they had survived unscarred. To have endured as much as they had was to suffer a disruption of personality more violent than anything experienced by our pre-war refugees.

They arrived at Carlisle in two RAF bombers and were taken by bus to Windermere. Of the two forms of transport, the bus was more comfortable because it had seats. The majority of the youngsters were between fourteen and nineteen, but there were a dozen who were under seven years of age. Out of the 300 there were only thirty girls.

A few were quickly diagnosed as carriers of tuberculosis. Other victims were identified after an intensive medical overhaul. About forty patients required isolation. But where? The Home Office had stipulated that infectious illness was a disqualification for entry to the country, so we were not to expect any help from that quarter. But the game was not lost. With typical enterprise Lola Hahn Warburg chased off to a sanatorium near Ashford, where she persuaded the doctor in charge to let her borrow an empty ward. All we had to provide were the nurses. We stayed for over a year until our patients had recovered to the stage where they were judged too noisy and boisterous to be in hospital. Those still needing medical treatment were moved to a hostel in Bishop's Stortford.

First impressions of Windermere, which was fairly Spartan by most standards, were ecstatic. One former occupant recalls: 'A tiny room with a bed, chest of drawers and a wardrobe. A room all to myself. Has anyone ever lived so luxuriously?' Clean sheets were a novelty; so was a toothbrush. As the dentist was soon to confirm, there were boys at Windermere who had not cleaned their teeth in five years.

There were two more transports. One went to Southampton, the other to Belfast. The idea was to accommodate all the youngsters in the reception centres for up to three months. In this time it was hoped to prepare them for family life or, in the case of the older teenagers, for independence. It was a tall order. A sense of security was not easily rediscovered. Kind words were suspect; gentleness was interpreted as weakness. When food was stolen from the kitchen, we had to remind ourselves that we were dealing with people who could not yet believe in the reality of the next meal. When there was fighting over the possession of a coat or a pair of shoes, we had to remember the rules of survival in a concentration camp. One boy bluntly admitted: 'The reason I'm alive is that I was strong enough to take a piece of bread from someone too weak to eat it.'

Leonard Montefiore was infinitely patient: 'They have been in contact with every kind of vice and wickedness the mind can conceive. For them, during the whole of their childhood, honesty was the very worst policy. It led immediately to destruction. How can they be expected to learn, in a short while, the reverse of the maxim taught them by bitter experience?' According to Leonard the first article of faith was perseverance. And he was right.

Where we made our breakthrough was in the classroom. Our young friends were not just tough, they were also highly intelligent. And they wanted to learn. It was as if they were trying to make up for lost time. Even now, all these years later, I confess to an enormous feeling of pride when I think of the camp orphans who, against all the odds, escaped the gas chambers and the firing squads to become no ordinary citizens, but leaders in their chosen occupations.

Shared experience – the achievement of having pulled through – created a powerful bond of comradeship. Unlike the pre-war refugees who gave every sign of wanting to put away the past, the children of the concentration camps had a need for a continuing association. No doubt many were seeking reassurance. Accustomed to a small, closed society, the world outside could be frightening in its complexity. But also, I fancy, there was an awareness that, as a community, they stood for something. Not one of them today would express such grand sentiments, but they knew then, as now, that they had fought a massive evil and won. It is surely open to me, as an outsider, to suggest that there is a message here for the rest of mankind.

The 45 Aid Society, with its highly exclusive membership, is still active today. One of the founder members and later chairman is Ben Helfgott, who was fifteen when he came here. He had spent all the war years in concentration camps. His mother and younger sister had died in 1942 in a mass murder of Jews. His father, from whom he was separated in September 1944, was shot trying to escape just a few days before the end of the war. After all this Ben went on to make a home and a success in business, raise a family and, for leisure, train as a weight-lifter, a sport which took him twice to the Olympics. Whenever we have touched on the big questions of life, his response has always been the same: 'I am by nature', he says, 'an incurable optimist.'

By the end of the 1940s, the work of the RCM had been merged with that of the Central British Fund, though Lord Gorell's guardianship, the focal point of the Movement, remained in force until 1959 when the last refugee child came of age. My involvement ceased when I went to America in 1948, but up to then I was a fixture on the merry-go-round of consultations to sort out the problems of what was still a substantial and often troublesome family.

There were girls who wanted to marry early (we looked for 'integrity and respectability' in potential husbands), girls who had to marry early and, sadly, a few girls who would have married but for the unannounced departure of their lovers.

A broken romance left Paula with a baby to care for on her own. She lived in a single room, and it soon became clear how she was earning her money. She had two more babies before she was twenty-one. The Movement arranged for adoption and tried counselling – God knows we tried counselling – but without getting anywhere. Then along came Brian. He knew the whole story, he said, but he still wanted to marry her and, as much to the point, she wanted to marry him. Thankfully, the file was closed.

There were boys who could not find work to match their talents, boys who thought they were underpaid for the work they were doing, and boys who tried to solve both problems by turning against the law. We represented Martin when he was arrested with a revolver (fortunately unloaded) and Herbert when he was unable to explain how he came to have not one but two gold watches in his pocket. But court appearances were infrequent and, to my knowledge, we never had to deal with a really serious crime.

Several hospital cases were serious, though here we could do little else but make frequent visits. Perhaps I should not minimize the contribution. The meeting of friends was a vital part of the treatment, particularly where youngsters had earlier experience of the pain of loneliness. Lola once told me about a girl she visited in a mental hospital. Each time Lola appeared she brought a bunch of flowers, which the girl took and held close for an hour or more. In this time she said not a single word. Even when, according to the doctors, she was showing signs of recovery, she and Lola never spoke to each other. But years later the girl, now a young woman, came to see Lola. Her greeting was a revelation. 'I shall never forget your visits.' she said. And she never did.

A Very Remarkable Surgeon

Aside from the prospect of sudden demise, London was not a bad place to spend the war. As ever, it helped to be able to buy a certain amount of comfort, like a suite at Claridge's for weekday residence. But please note I did say comfort – not luxury. Wartime restrictions were rigorously enforced. It was as if the staff was getting its own back for years of genuflecting to the gentry. Only once did I openly defy the rules. After walking back from the office in pouring rain, I demanded a full bath – not the regulation six-inch splash about – as an essential antidote to the onset of pneumonia. The housemaid refused, but the manager, bless him, took my side. It was democracy in action – and in Claridge's of all places – though I confess I influenced a favourable result by shivering and sneezing rather a lot.

Claridge's was only a walk from the office, which meant that I could work the hours I needed without worrying about getting home in the blackout. That was my official reason for staying there. Unofficially, I enjoyed the thrill of being at the centre of things. Like all other London hotels, Claridge's was under military occupation. At times it was like living in a barracks, albeit a very superior one. I cannot say that I was ever invited to the inner councils of allied strategy, but I did enjoy the attention of bright young officers who seemed to find me an agreeable dinner companion.

It was all such an invigorating change from Melbury Road, where my soured relationship with Norman had set the mood of almost permanent depression. When Norman joined up, it was like a signal that the marriage had finally ended. After he was posted to Burton-on-Trent to run a royal ordnance depot, we saw little of each other. With the children at boarding-school, Melbury Road lost all interest for me. I locked the door and never went back.

Neville, too, was in uniform, in the RAF. He was sent to North Wales, of all places. I felt badly about this until he was given a job at the Ministry of Production with an office on the Embankment and a flat off Piccadilly. A few months later I moved out of Claridge's and into an apartment in Arlington House, just across the road from Neville.

By now everyone who knew us well also knew that Neville and I were having an affair. But still the family resisted the urge to quiz me about my private life. I was grateful and at the same time nervous. I was convinced that they were waiting for me to take the initiative with Simon.

I was presented with a golden opportunity, which I fluffed, when Simon told me he wanted to talk about the children. I went along with a prepared speech on how the interests of all would best be served if we frankly acknowledged the breakdown of my marriage. But Simon had his own speech to deliver. Characteristically, it was short and to the point.

'I want you to go to America. Take Ann and Simone with you.'

'Why?'

'It's not safe here.'

'What about the others? Is the rest of the family going?'

'No, not yet, anyway. You're the advance guard.'

'Well, I don't want to go.'

'Why not?'

Now here was my best chance yet of telling Simon that I wanted to stay because I was in love with Neville and planned to marry him. But this would have shifted the argument on to my weak ground, allowing Simon the chance of winning by exploiting my sense of guilt. So instead I replied: 'I've no intention of becoming a refugee until I'm forced. Anyway, I've got work to do!' I don't think Simon had ever expected his youngest sister to invoke work as a justification for anything. He must have been impressed, for there were no further suggestions for getting me out of the country.

When at last I did pluck up enough courage to admit to Simon my intention of divorcing Norman, there was a most fearsome row. Was I not ashamed to be the first of the Marks to enter the divorce courts? (No, not particularly.) Had I thought of the effect on the children? (Yes, and I could not believe that they would thank us for propping up an unhappy marriage.) Was I prepared to face the scandal? Oh, that was the difficult one. I did worry about the gossips and their power to turn friends and family against one. I had spent much of my life trying to open doors. The last thing I wanted now was for them to slam back in my face.

I took strength from Becky and Miriam, who weighed in on my behalf, and from Neville, who charmed his way over the barricades. He did it by a combination of good humour and straight talking, though he was blunt only up to a point – the point being Simon's level of tolerance. It was uncanny how Neville could judge so precisely how much Simon would take and then tailor his conversation accordingly. It was a diplomatic skill he used to good effect throughout his life.

Concentrating so hard on winning over Simon, I made the mistake of not paying enough attention to Norman. After agreeing in principle to a divorce, Norman appeared to banish the matter from his mind, thus giving me reason to believe that he would fit in with the usual pattern of events. But when it came to arranging the messy business of proving grounds for a divorce – in those days we had to have a sworn statement from a private detective to prove adultery – Norman flatly refused to act as the guilty party. And who, you might ask, could blame him? Well, just about everyone as it turned out. The well-established convention, long before the dawn of women's liberation, was for the man always to accept the blame for the failure of a marriage. To do otherwise was to offend against the traditional image of woman as the loyal and obedient servant. For a man to stray was natural and forgivable, for a woman to stray was unnatural and unforgivable. Though widely regarded as hypocritical nonsense, the rules of marriage and divorce were sustained by strong social forces, which I was not eager to offend. So started a long and weary argument with Norman to persuade him to do the decent thing. In this unequal struggle (Norman, for the first time in his life, resolutely refused to budge), I wasted a lot of time, a few tears and a fortune in lawyers' fees.

Meanwhile, there was a war to be fought. I got over my fear of bombs after the first air-raid warning. I was at Bassett House with the children when I heard the siren wailing over the countryside like a lost soul. I concentrated my nervousness on Ann, who was returning from a visit to friends. When she arrived home safely, it was like a promise that no bombs would fall on us. Even afterwards when we discovered that we had agonized over a false alarm and that the skies had not been crowded with engines of destruction, the experience was somehow reassuring. Maybe our chances were not quite so bad as we had imagined.

In London, I seldom went into the shelters. 'You mustn't worry about me,' I told an American friend whose response to the siren was to rush me underground.

'Hell, I'm not,' he shouted. 'But what happens if you're killed and I escape. Your family will never forgive me.' His logic was unbeatable.

My refusal to contemplate destruction from the air was shared by at least one member of staff. Ripley, the butler, maintained an air of serene indifference to matters that were not immediately relevant to his domestic duties. One jolly weekend in the country when up to a dozen guests sat down to dinner, Ripley served everyone in order before arriving at the head of the table to announce in his grandest manner, 'I thought you might like to know, Madam. There was an air-raid warning ten minutes ago.' I have never seen a room clear so fast.

The antithesis to Ripley was my cook-housekeeper, who looked after me when I moved into the London flat. Alice was a tiny, energetic Cockney who, according to the children, made the best Lancashire hotpot and, according to me, drank more gin than was good for her. Come the late evening Alice would appear in her ARP helmet to announce her departure to the roof, where she spent much of the night looking out for enemy bombers through an alcoholic haze. She knew enough not to report her sightings to me until the morning. The exception came towards the end of the war when, so overwhelmed by what she had seen, she rushed down to my bedroom to announce the appearance of 'shooting stars'. 'Up there in the sky they are,' she declared, waving vaguely at the ceiling, 'shooting stars sent by that Hitler.' I told her firmly not to be so silly and to go to bed. The following day I had to apologize. Alice had spotted the first flying bombs!

During my time at Claridge's once the staff had realized that I was not a heavy sleeper who needed an extra loud knock to get me out of bed, I enjoyed a certain reputation for foolhardy bravery. The illusion was dispelled, however, when in the middle of a quiet tea, I came close to a horror so abominable that my screams were heard throughout the building. Waiters and serving maids rushed to help, but not one of them was able to catch the mouse.

If not at Bloomsbury House or at Claridge's, my London friends could usually find me at the Balfour Services Club where I was chairman of the house committee. The Club was set up at the beginning of the war by a small group of FWZ ladies led by Tina Bloch. The idea was to provide a second home for Jewish servicemen who were strangers to London. It proved so popular that in a few months we outgrew the Rose Hertz Hall in Woburn Place (which anyway had been made unsafe by bomb damage) and moved into two houses in Portland Place. A letter from Otto Schiff, written in early 1946, summarizes our achievement in culinary terms. In an average week we served 14,000 hot beverages, 4,000 main meals, 730 breakfasts, 5,000 subsidiary meals and 5,000 afternoon teas. By the time the Balfour Club closed, I felt I had all the training and experience to run a top-flight hotel.

Soon after the beginning of the war, when the arrangement with the owner of Bassett House came to an end, I started looking for another house that would suit me as a country retreat – and as a real home, since my new accommodation in London had a distinctly temporary feel about it. I found what I wanted in Saint Hill, a grey stone mansion which, in later years, was to acquire a certain notoriety as the British headquarters of the Scientologists. It had a magnificent terrace overlooking the Sussex Downs and a flat roof which we had to camouflage with green paint.

Saint Hill was not far from East Grinstead, then a small market-town known outside its own boundaries as a place you drive through on the way to Brighton. In the absence of historical monuments or other distinctive features the town's pride and joy was the cottage hospital. This was not the usual red-brick relic with lavatory tiling in the corridors and bars up at the windows, but a fine new building designed to combine efficiency and comfort. Financed chiefly by the Kindersleys and other wealthy families in the area, the hospital opened in 1936 to a fanfare of self-congratulation.

But by the time I was introduced to the Queen Victoria Hospital, in early 1940, the euphoria had long since passed away. Now there was much shaking of hands and dark mutterings about troubles caused by 'outside interference'. The source of the dissatisfaction was the way in which East Grinstead had been swept along by emergency regulations. It was only to be expected that the Queen Victoria would be made a casualty centre for London; a little surprising that it should be asked to specialize in burns and facial injuries, a branch of medicine outside the range of a cottage hospital; but totally objectionable that the job of setting up and managing the operation should go to a young and pushy Harley Street surgeon whose sole claim to fame was a talent for beautifying rich ladies. This, as I was soon to discover, was a total misjudgement of a most extraordinary man.

Archie McIndoe was a New Zealander of Scottish ancestry, a scholarship boy who worked his way from medical school to the Mayo Clinic (where the Americans trained him to be an abdominal surgeon) and then to a smart and fashionable practice in London. His partner was the country's leading plastic surgeon, Sir Harold Gillies. The two were distantly related, but there was no hint of nepotism in Archie's rise to fortune. Gillies was a hard-headed businessman who let Archie prove his talent, by coming out top in the Royal College of Surgeons exams, before giving him his chance.

The older man was also a notable eccentric, whose effrontery could send patients running in panic. 'How dare you come to see me looking like that,' he roared at a society lady, who had just emerged transformed from the hairdresser's. 'Come back when your head is its natural colour.'

By contrast, Archie was always friendly and approachable. He could be firm but never offensive. His hard time with Gillies came when patients showed a preference for the newcomer. 'He's good,' Gillies told a colleague, 'but not that good. Not yet.'

By his mid-thirties, Archie was counted as one of the five top plastic surgeons. He had a large income, a smart flat opposite the London Clinic and a promise from Gillies that, if all went well, he could expect to succeed the great man. What he missed was the respect of his peers. For the medical establishment, plastic surgery was merely applied cosmetics, a simple matter of lifting breasts and straightening noses, not at all the sort of activity that would add lustre to the profession. Gillies, who had practised his skills on shell victims from the First World War, knew differently. With another war expected, he encouraged Archie to take over from him as consultant surgeon to the RAF. It was the closest that Archie ever got to military rank.

In March 1939 the Queen Victoria Hospital was allocated its wartime role as a centre for burns and facial injuries. Archie was asked if he would take charge, should the need arise. Before deciding, he motored down to view the place. He liked the position – it was a convenient run from his private practice – and he liked the building. He called it 'a nice little hospital on the outskirts of a nice little town'. He was not so sure about the staff and the managers. They were equally uncertain about him; 'He bowled in as if he owned the hospital and started lecturing everyone on how to do their jobs,' complained a stalwart of the management committee.

'It's true,' said Archie when, later, I got his side of the story. 'I was a bit heavy-handed, but there wasn't any time to waste.' He was right. Once he agreed to take on the Queen Victoria there was much work to do, very quickly. Equally, the burghers of East Grinstead were not easily persuaded of the need for urgency. The threat of terror bombing on London creating thousands of casualties seemed unreal to any except those at the centre of the danger zone. When, after the first few months of the war the Nazi onslaught had still not materialized, the tendency was to accuse the authorities of crying wolf. What was the desperate hurry for the extra wards, new equipment and drugs, and intensive training? It all cost so much money, which the Queen Victoria did not have. At one acrimonious management meeting the treasurer reported a balance of just £27. He left no one in doubt as to whom he blamed for the collapse of prudent administration.

But Archie soon made amends, by proving that he could raise money almost as fast as he could spend it. Spurning the usual charity flag day and garden parties, he made straight for the wealthy set – the Dewars of whisky fame, the Kindersleys and the Marks. He gave us his best bedside manner – the sweet charm of a man of the world who was used to making decisions, yours as well as his own. I was immediately attracted to Archie; not as a prospective lover (the rumours though gaining credence by repetition were totally unfounded), but as a true, loyal friend who could always be relied upon for sympathetic advice. I was able to talk freely to Archie in a way that was impossible with others, even Neville who refused to acknowledge problems he did not understand.

The difference between them showed up most obviously in their contacts with Simone and Ann. With children of his own Neville was not keen to take on extra parental duties. He was always jovial with the girls, but kept his distance like a visiting uncle who did not expect to see them more than once a year. Archie was quite the opposite. Though, as an occasional visitor, he saw less of Simone and Ann, his readiness to listen and his sixth sense of knowing when to listen made him the natural father figure. The relationship continued long after the war. He was at his best (and I was no help at all) when Simone was escaping from a horrendous first marriage.

If turning to Archie was a family habit, I am pleased to think that he returned the compliment. We had early warning of his trouble – marital and professional. When the problems could be solved by money, we never failed him. Archie was equally generous with his valuable asset, his time. I recall especially his readiness to help on cases involving our young refugees. When the children from the concentration camps arrived, Archie was there to remove the brand marks from their arms.

I learn from the records that my first contribution to the Queen Victoria – a modest gift – was in late 1939. I cannot now remember why the cash was needed, but I guess it had something to do with brightening up the new wards which had been built to the rear of the hospital. These were three long, low wooden huts which, inside, were painted a sickly cream and brown. They were fitted with cast-iron beds and a minimum of other furniture made out of cheap plywood. The overall effect was infinitely depressing.

At Archie's insistence, the welfare committee, of which I was a novice member, embarked on 'operation facelift'. Out went the old-fashioned bedsteads, in came bright wooden frames with soft springs. The cream and brown paintwork was blotted out by a new coat of green and pink. Curtains went up; official notices warning of the dreadful consequences of rule breaking came down. The strip of land outside was transformed from a rubble tip to a well-tended garden.

The purpose, explained Archie, was to create an environment in which patients could feel the warmth of human contact. Plastic surgery could go a long way towards reconstructing the damaged body; what it could not, of itself, achieve was the rejuvenation of a damaged personality. Pleasant and cheerful surroundings were the prerequisite for the gradual reintroduction of the burns victim into the real world.

Archie's theory of treating the whole person was soon to be put to the test. He took up his appointment as Medical Superintendent on day one of the war. For the first few months, his services were not over-extended. By the end of 1939 only seventy or so burns cases had been admitted to the Queen Victoria. Casualties from Dunkirk were followed by victims of the first bombs on London, but nowhere near as many as the doom merchants had prophesied.

Then we were into the Battle of Britain and the panic rush started. Of all the services, the RAF suffered the most burns injuries. Fighter pilots were particularly vulnerable. This was because the petrol tank on a Spitfire or Hurricane was at the front of the aircraft. If it was set alight, the forward motion of the plane brought the flames back into the cockpit. From the beginning to the end of the war 4,500 British airmen were treated by plastic surgeons. Most of the serious cases came to East Grinstead. Of the 600 or so in Archie's own special charge, at least 200 needed a total reconstruction of face and hands.

I often wonder if the young men who took their joy of flying into the war ever knew what they were risking. An objective answer is impossible. For the survivors, what they experienced and what they expected has inevitably overlapped, blurring the truth. We can say only that the schoolboy dream of teaming up with Biggles to chase the Hun across a clear blue sky, along with the other romantic illusions of aerial warfare, were soon dispelled by cruel reality.

But having proved their courage in battle, airmen with ravaged bodies were asked to demonstrate another and, I believe, a higher level of bravery. It took the form of a long and painful submission to surgical skill. Skin grafting consisted of the cutting away and replacement of dead tissue with healthy skin from another part of the patient's body, usually the abdomen or chest. Similarly, pieces of bone were taken from the hip or shin to rebuild vital facial features.

Starting with new eyelids and lips, so that the patient could at least sleep and eat, the repair of a badly burned face could take up to forty operations over four or five years. For many, it was not the operating table – the slab – that bothered them so much as the waiting between operations and the tension of not knowing if, in the end, the surgeon would work the miracle for them. How would they be judged when the time came to face the world – and for the world to face them? This is where Archie's social skills came into play. It was all a question of building self-confidence. Our efforts to create a homely mood in the wards was only a beginning.

In 1941, the welfare committee was reconstituted under Archie's chairmanship. I was one of the six members. We enjoyed great freedom: to raise as much money as we could in whatever way we thought fit and, within reason, to spend it. In theory, we needed permission from the management board for any project of over £100, but, if the cause was dear to Archie's heart, he encouraged us to spend first and ask for approval afterwards.

My best effort at fund-raising for the Queen Victoria was £4,000 from one evening in the cinema. Charity premieres are old-hat nowadays, but in the war their rarity value helped towards a good turnout for the right sort of entertainment. The obvious ingredient was star names in a not-too-demanding show. Something light and exhilarating was called for. I turned first to the live theatre. A couple of musical comedies were ready to come in: one a vehicle for Jack Buchanan, the other called *Something in the Air*, an excuse for bringing together on stage the husband and wife team, Jack Hulbert and Cicely Courtneidge. I would happily have taken either, but there were too many uncertainties – on timing and on the availability of theatres. In the West End of the early 1940s, you seldom knew what would be on from one week to the next.

The cinema, I was told, was more predictable. Paramount had just completed a film which looked to be ideal: *Lady in the Dark*, an adaptation of a Broadway musical. The story was by Moss Hart, the music by Kurt Weill and the lyrics by Ira Gershwin. The stars were Ginger Rogers and Ray Milland. What more could we want? Quite a lot, as it turned out, because the film itself was a disappointment – too many slow misty dream sequences. The studio must have spent a fortune on dry ice. Still, our night out at the Plaza cinema in Regent Street was a sell-out. And for those who did not take too strongly to the main feature, there were compensating amusements – a technicolor cartoon featuring Little Lulu, a newsreel, favourite tunes from The Skyrockets and an RAF dance orchestra from No. 1 Balloon Centre (by permission of the officer commanding). What's more, the Germans stayed away. Not a single bomb dropped on London during the performance.

Back at the hospital, meanwhile, the revolution had started. Rules put up merely to support military convention were knocked aside. The best interests of the patients was now the first consideration. To demonstrate the verdict beyond all doubt there was a wild ceremony, known as the burning of the blues: the hospital uniforms – long white shirt, red tie, blue jacket and trousers – so hated for their institutional uniformity, were collected, taken and hurled on to a splendid bonfire.

Sanctioning what was doubtless a court-martial offence, Archie was glad he had not succumbed to the vanity of military rank. At the Queen Victoria, he was the boss, and the powers – military and civil service – were not allowed to forget it. If he detected incompetence or injustice, he was prepared, as he put it, 'to kick up hell' until the matter was put right. He did so when his anaesthetist, Russell Davies, complained of the arbitrary way in which disability pensions were awarded – 100 per cent for the loss of both eyes, for instance, but only forty per cent for the loss of one eye. Why just forty per cent? Who decided? In the absence of logical answers, Russell worked out a new scale of payments which gave many more patients the right to a full pension. Archie took it to Whitehall and refused to budge until he was convinced that the message had got across. 'They saw reason,' he reported, after his excursion. I thought it was more likely that they saw stars. Wanting to do more for his patients, but unable to spare his medical staff who were already working up to a fourteen-hour day, Archie recruited a full-time father figure and cheer-leader.

Edward Blacksell, ever after known as Blackie, came without any terms of reference: 'I was told to report to the education officer. But he didn't know what to do with me and I certainly didn't know what to do with him.' He was a school-teacher, recruited into the RAF to be a physical training instructor. Like all the best of his profession he was an inveterate optimist. He soon came up with a few uplifting ideas: beer was put on tap – in the wards; a radiogram was installed – with records to suit all tastes; and nurses were introduced who were pretty and did not mind having their bottoms pinched. It was quite a party.

The feeling of camaraderie produced by this bizarre set-up was given positive form by a club – the Guinea Pigs. It started as a boozy joke, but like so much else at the Queen Victoria, the humour had an underlying seriousness. 'Stick together', Archie told them, 'nothing is impossible.' And the Guinea Pigs took him at his word. They still have a yearly get-together – at East Grinstead, of course. Forty years later, Blackie was still on hand, though more as the problem solver than the impresario.

Getting out – to the cinema, to shops, to people's homes – was an essential part of the treatment at the Queen Victoria. But scarred faces and shrivelled limbs could shock the uninitiated. Archie wanted his

Guinea Pigs to be accepted and not have to bear the hurt of rejection. So he urged, 'Invite them into your homes, make them welcome, show them they're wanted.'

At Saint Hill, the Guinea Pigs came to dinner – and stayed on. We gave over half the rooms as a convalescent wing of the Queen Victoria. Eight to ten patients were there at any one time, together with one or two medical staff who used Saint Hill as a bolthole, a place to relax. Archie and Blackie had their own rooms, which they fled to when they wanted to get away from it all.

If other of my friends visited and did not like what they saw, they knew exactly what they had to do. I surprised myself, as someone who tends to veer away from sickness, how quickly I became accustomed to deformity. I was genuinely taken aback when, at Claridge's, I earned a rebuke for causing offence to the rest of the clientele. All I had done was to introduce a party of friends to the dining-room, who just happened to be Guinea Pigs. When I realized what the fuss was about I went to find the manager. The poor man was properly ashamed. 'Do you realize,' I thundered, 'if it wasn't for these boys there wouldn't be a Claridge's. Now, tell the staff to treat them like dukes.'

Sometimes there was trouble the other way. A naturally boisterous group of young men who were encouraged to keep their spirits up were bound, occasionally, to get out of hand. When it happened, Archie descended like the mighty avenger. He had numerous punishments to inflict, the most serious being a return to hospital blues, a few sets of which he had saved from the flames. Only once did good humour fail to win through. Some Polish airmen chose Saint Hill to give vent to anti-Semitism. The response from Archie was immediate. He refused to have them back at the Queen Victoria. Though, as far as I know, without any Jewish family connections, Archie was always ready to spring to our defence. It might have been self-interest, of course, but if money had been his only concern there were plenty of non-Jewish sources he could, and did, utilize. I believe he was a tolerant person who found it difficult to understand intolerance. He came to me once with a letter from the officer in charge of a retraining centre for injured airmen. Archie had encouraged me to supply some names of people who might have helped the centre in the way we were helping the Queen Victoria. The offer had been refused because 'all the ladies mentioned are of a certain persuasion'. The correspondent assumed that Archie would go along with the view that 'it is best to avoid cliques'.

'Can you believe it?' he asked me. Sadly, I could believe it, very easily. Archie sent a curt reply. 'Just forget it,' he wrote.

Even with increased funds from government and private sources, improvisation was still the rule. The saline bath treatment was a case in point and one remembered by every wartime inmate of the Queen Victoria. Archie was convinced that grafts would take more quickly and successfully if the wounded man bathed in salt water. The evidence for this came from the First World War, when surgeons noticed that burns on sailors who had been rescued from the sea healed much faster than average. Archie's views were not immediately accepted by the military, who held to an alternative treatment: a mix of tannic acid, silver nitrate and gentian violet, which stopped infection but hardened the dressings so that they were difficult to remove. Also, the concoction smelt horrible.

Knowing how long it would take for the War Wounds Committee to change course, Archie simply followed his own reasoning. What was needed? Just an old bath tub and a little amateur plumbing. Patient and stretcher were slung over the bath by two robust attendants, who gently lowered their cargo into the warm brine. The improvisation worked brilliantly. With only minor refinements, such as the replacement of taps with a shower which was easier to handle and did not get in the way of the stretcher, the saline bath saw out the war.

In their association with the Queen Victoria – a cottage hospital no longer – the people of East Grinstead had a lot to contend with. They coped rather well – not just with the wild young Britishers, but with Canadians, Americans, French, Poles and Czechs. The cosmopolitan look was out of character for a town long identified with the Colonel Blimp brand of conservatism, but stories of prejudice against foreigners were rare. I remember only the distressed comment of a parent whose daughter had sampled the pleasure of a Gaelic romance: 'I do sometimes wonder if it's wise to let them out.' But she hastily corrected any impression of bias: 'I'm sure our boys are just as bad.' There was no argument with her on that score.

Of all the Guinea Pigs my soft spot was for the Americans and Canadians. They came here – to Europe – to help us, yet never once did they resent the sacrifice. I made some fine friends, including one,

Lieutenant Ozzie Friedgut, who paid me the great compliment of naming his baby daughter after me. When the patients went home, or back to their units, they nearly all proved to be great letter writers. I was never short of news, even from those who found themselves in restrained circumstances. 'Here's another fine mess I've got myself into,' begins a card from an Italian prisoner-of-war camp. When, for one reason or another, the boys were not able to keep in touch, I invariably heard from their parents, wives or girlfriends – or, in one case, from a wife and a girlfriend, both of whom assumed the exclusive right to write on behalf of their loved one.

But for anyone who lived through those days at East Grinstead, the Guinea Pig who first comes to mind is Richard Hillary. He stayed at Saint Hill on and off over a period of about eighteen months. In so many ways he represented the triumph and the tragedy of his generation of fliers. Stepping out from Trinity with all the advantages – an enquiring mind, good looks and a determination to make his mark – he was a natural for the RAF. Not so much typical of fighter pilots, he was the epitome of what all fighter pilots wanted to be.

But the flames which took away half his face also destroyed his deeper image of himself. It was not unusual for Guinea Pigs to lose their reason for living – and, gradually, to rediscover it as body and personality healed as one. Richard Hillary wanted more – a new identity, stronger than the old – to compensate for his terrible scars. He eschewed emotion. He used arrogance and cynicism to turn away sympathy, and to obliterate self-pity he kept a diary – a close, sharply factual record of everything that happened to him in the Queen Victoria. It was a fine piece of writing. Published as *The Last Enemy*, it became a best-seller. The public proclaimed him a war hero, but he was a hero not everyone wanted to know at first hand. When he went to America to promote the allied cause, he was told to stand back in case he frightened the raw recruits. Real or imagined slights battered what he now realized was a fragile reconstruction of his confidence. He could have taken refuge at East Grinstead, as Archie pressed him to do, but this was too much like a retreat. There was only one other choice: he went back to the RAF as a flier. And that is how he died – as a flier. When I heard the news, someone, I think it might have been Blackie, murmured: 'The war hero is dead. Long live the war hero.'

And the legend did live on. Years later I was reading an article about Archie and the Guinea Pigs in *Reader's Digest*. There was a mention of Richard Hillary, who was commemorated as one shot down in action. They just had to write that. In fact, he was killed in a routine training flight. It was almost certainly a case of pilot error.

The memory of old age compresses the years. Though I have kept in close contact with the Guinea Pigs and have helped a few of them with their careers, for many of them it must have been after rather than during the war that I got to know them well. I was at Saint Hill only at the weekends, and then often fleetingly. But Ann and Simone spent their school holidays there, in Guinea Pig company. Simone remembers a sunny afternoon, out with one of the convalescents, walking, as she told me, 'hand in burnt hand'. When I saw Ann, a beautiful girl, just about to leave school, dancing with a badly burned Guinea Pig I could not help thinking, 'What would I say if she wants to marry him?' I never gave myself a direct answer, but the question kept popping back into my mind because by mid-war I was seeing more of the Guinea Pigs' wives and girlfriends than of the Guinea Pigs themselves. I was edged in their direction by Blackie, who felt that the women's role was being understated. I knew what he meant. It took a lot of courage for a young girl, in the first excitement of life, to recognize the commitment of living with a badly injured man. A few were quite unable to meet the challenge – and mercifully accepted their limitation early on. They were not thanked at the time, but I remain convinced that for our boys a broken romance was easiest to take when there were lots of friends together to help absorb the blow.

I was gratified to find that most women just took it for granted that they would go on, somehow. The resilience of my sex never ceases to amaze me. How much help I was able to give, I cannot say. Awkward in giving advice on personal relationships even at the best of times, I could at least listen. Sometimes, that's all it took.

Teenage friendships apart, these cannot have been happy years for the children. They missed Norman and saw little enough of me. Never the domesticated mother, I realize now that I was too ready to use the war as an excuse for absentee parenthood. Even that I mishandled. I tried to keep to the habit of writing to the girls once a week in term, but if I was rushed I dictated a few lines to my secretary, the formidable Grace Slater, who tactfully filled in the gaps. There came the day when a typed letter for Simone presented to me for signature was tailed, as most of my other correspondence, 'Yours sincerely, Elaine'! I ought to have had the letter redone, but we were in a hurry so I just crossed out the formalities and wrote in 'Mummy'. The hurt silence carried all the way from Cheltenham Ladies' College to Saint Hill.

The war made Archie. It may also, indirectly, have been the death of him. Day after day, he worked himself to a standstill, beginning in the operating theatre at eight in the morning and finishing not before nine or ten at night. His style of operating – always letting the patient know what was being done to him and why, openly inviting suggestions and criticism – increased the strain of acting the Maestro. He was backed by a dedicated team – John Hunter and Russell Davies, his anaesthetists, Jill Mullins, an indispensable theatre sister – but they too felt the burden of incessant labour. By the end of the war, John Hunter, a diabetic for whom the bottle was the symbol of relaxation, and Jill Mullins, who managed a high blood pressure without touching a drop, were both showing the obvious signs of wear and tear.

Archie too saw the view from the other side of the consultant's desk. In 1943 he developed Dupuytren's Contracture, a fibrous growth in the palm of the hand which pulls the fingers inwards towards the wrist. An operation was essential, though Archie took some time to make the inevitable decision. 'Remember,' he told the surgeon, 'you stand between me and the bankruptcy court.' He may have been joking, but when he repeated the story to me he was not smiling.

It was while Archie was recovering from his operation that East Grinstead had its worst night of the war. A German raider, unloading a stack of bombs over the centre of the town, scored a direct hit on the Whitehall cinema. Over 100 people were killed and twice as many seriously injured. The hospital worked round the clock, and Archie rushed back from London to help with the emergency cases.

To the physical pressures endured by Archie must be added the emotional problems of an unsatisfactory marriage. Andonia was a loyal but otherwise uninspiring partner. In their early days together in New Zealand, when Archie won a scholarship for a single person to study at the Mayo Clinic, she selflessly agreed to stay at home while her husband of less than a year set off for the other side of the world. The separation was shorter than either of them expected because the Mayo Clinic relented when Archie confessed all; still,

Andonia's gesture proved a fine regard for his career.

She was compliant again when Archie packed her and the children off to America at the beginning of the war. It was, he said, for safety's sake that he did what so many other wealthy families were doing (what Simon had tried to make me do), but he was undoubtedly pleased to be free of the bother of keeping up pretences. Certainly he was irritated when, in 1944, Andonia announced her intention of returning. Archie did his best to dissuade her. By then he was enjoying the life of a celebrity. As a single man, if only by force of circumstances, much of the hero worship he attracted came from the ladies. Archie showed himself not to be averse to their attention. There was also a close relationship with the attractive Jill Mullins, which did wonders for his peace of mind. But with Andonia back, the flirting and the affairs had to stop.

Archie stood the strain for a few months. Then the rows got too much for him. Andonia refused to get involved with the hospital, hated going to parties and complained when Archie stayed too long with his patients. As a result he spent even less time at home. On several occasions at Saint Hill, he spoke openly about the possibility of divorce, but worried about his children and about Andonia herself, who was too ready to seek consolation in a bottle. There was also the question of a knighthood. Archie knew he was in line for an honour and had set his heart on it, but a divorce could well damage his chances.

They split up in late 1946. Andonia went to live in Kensington in a flat Archie bought for her; later she settled in Brighton. At East Grinstead meanwhile, Jill Mullins was back in favour. Neville and I were convinced that they would marry. But the final chapter of Archie's love life was to turn out quite differently from the way we predicted.

The last of Archie's trinity of problems was money. Before the war he had made a good living from his private practice. By comparison, his official salary at the Queen Victoria was a pittance. He did not have time to make up the difference by rushing off to the London Clinic (though for a long period, he did try).

So what did Archie gain from the war? A much enhanced reputation, of that there can be no doubt. While not the greatest of technical innovators, he, more than any other individual, advanced plastic surgery to the front rank of medical achievement. He knew what it took to bring a human being back from the edge of destruction.

Public recognition, affirmed by the award of a knighthood in 1947, helped to enrich the Harley Street practice which Archie was already using to good effect to restore the family fortune. Stars of the gossip columns lined up for his services. It was to Archie that the rising young film actress, Kay Kendall, owed thanks for her impish nose (previously it had been a little too plump to match her coquettish personality). When Ava Gardner fell off a horse, naturally her first thought was to call in Archie to remove the bruise from her face; and when the Duchess of Windsor tripped over a suitcase, who else but Archie could be trusted to repair the gash on her cheek?

The war ending was not, as some people anticipated, the signal for Archie to depart from East Grinstead. There was still a job to be done – Guinea Pig operations continued well into 1947 – but, anyway, Archie had invested too much of his life in the Queen Victoria to cut away easily.

As his reputation had grown, so had the hospital – in size as well as in status. In July 1944 a new wing – financed by the Canadians, built by the Royal Canadian Engineers and staffed, for the duration, by the Royal Canadian Air Force – was dedicated to 'the gallant young men whose wounds have brought them here and to the surgeons, nurses and staff who have cared for them'.

A yet more ambitious project was the American wing. Containing five operating theatres, the total cost was in the region of £100,000. The entire sum was donated by the US British War Relief Association after some desperate lobbying it must be said, since the original sum agreed had been smaller by two-thirds.

On the drawing-board was a new nurses' home, a children's wing, maternity centre and a rehabilitation centre. This last item was to be the fulfilment of the McIndoe grand plan: to provide a treatment which went beyond the mere physical needs of the patient to the deeper psychological problems of re-entering society. But Archie was no longer in charge. The new labour government and its radical Minister of Health saw to that.

Archie hated the very idea of a national health service. His arguments against it were, he said, practical not political: 'You wait; the civil servants will end up running the show.' When this happened, the GPs would submit to a form-filling routine, making their livings by pushing through as many bob-a-nob consultations as they could cram into a day without worrying much about the quality of treatment. The debate was hotting up. 'And what's more,' roared Archie at anyone for whom his first prognosis failed to make the required impact, 'all the best doctors will move south. You know how it was before the war. If you were in an industrial town, you gave a good cheap service to the community because you made a bit from your wealthy private patients. Now, all that's got to stop. So why should any doctor want to stay in a poor area?'

Supporters of national health, like Blackie and Russell Davies who, at this point, chipped in with idealists' notions of professional responsibility, were given a final cold blast of reality – or cynicism, depending upon your point of view. 'Well, you'll see. You'll see how it works out.'

I sometimes wonder how the antagonists might have adapted their views in the light of experience. No doubt Archie would have come round to the virtues of free medical treatment as of right, but in my view his fears for an over-bureaucratized service have been wholly justified. The strongest proponent of national health could hardly deny the invidious influence of top-heavy administration on the doctor-patient relationship. The right of a sick person to be treated as an intelligent and sensitive being was at the heart of Archie's philosophy. He would have fought like mad to keep the principle alive, but I doubt that even he would have succeeded against the massed army of penpushers.

In the first year of the Attlee administration Archie encouraged the hospital management boards, of which I was now a member, to believe that the government might be persuaded to exclude the Queen Victoria from its nationalization plans. Quite why we should be given special dispensation was never clear to me, but I went along with the campaign to the extent of encouraging Neville to set up contacts with Labour ministers who had worked alongside him at the Ministry of Production. We had some success. Sir Stafford Cripps was persuaded by Archie to relax the rules by which injured servicemen were required to leave the military – and so lose their only income – after a certain time. Henceforth long-term patients would not be discharged from the services until their treatment was complete.

Discussions with the Ministry of Health were equally rewarding. When the Marks family – in this instance represented by Simon,

Tilly and myself – let it be known that we were thinking of setting up three Fellowships in plastic surgery, the Ministry was quick to agree to financing three more Fellowships to the same value.

But try as he might, Archie was unable to get through to Aneuran Bevan, the standard bearer of social security who was in charge of housing, health and local government. Even a spot of emotive lobbying at Westminster by a party of Guinea Pigs secured no more than a sympathetic, but non-committal, hearing from Bevan's wife, Jennie Lee. In truth, events were moving too fast and too powerfully for an individual or small group to influence their course. Bevan had decided that for the health service to flourish, the hospital had to be brought under state control. The Queen Victoria would not be an exception.

The change of regime was delayed, by parliamentary procedure and administrative preparation, until July 1948. 'There was an atmosphere of mourning,' reported the local paper on the last meeting of the board, but I can't vouch for this personally. By then I was in America with Neville, doing my level best to promote British exports – another uphill task.

Roving Ambassador

Neville's divorce came through in 1941; mine in 1943. We were married, quietly, in a registry office the following year. We made no grand announcement of our plans, not even to the children. With Neville already part of the family scene, an elaborate wedding celebration seemed inappropriate.

Between us and the children there remained a distance forced on them by conflicting loyalties. Peter and Anthony were close to their mother, Ann and Simone to their father. Possibly, we might all have joined hands if Neville and I had stretched out a bit further, but we were short on parental confidence.

For some time Ann found it difficult to talk to Neville, who interpreted her silence as rejection. Simone made more of an effort but, as the younger sister still feeling her way into the adult world, she did not take well to Neville's love of stirring up a good argument, usually about subjects she thought were not worth worrying about. It was the same with Peter, then a shy young man whose leaning towards the quiet life made him a poor foil for Neville's provocation. Only with Anthony, whose sense of the outrageous was already well advanced, did Neville feel on equal terms.

There was little that Neville would not forgive Anthony, which was fortunate because with Anthony there was much to forgive. Only once was there a total breakdown in relations. It came, years later, when Anthony rang to tell his father 'some good news and some bad news'.

'What's the good news?'

'You're a grandfather.'

'But you're not married.'

'That's the bad news.'

Usually each gave as good as he got. Anthony's unauthorized, probably illegal, excursion from Eton to London on a motor-cycle, which he parked by the kerb outside our flat at Orchard Court, stunned Neville but only for a moment. As the proud young adventurer mounted the steps, Neville extended a £5 note to the

115

doorman and pointed to the bike. 'Get rid of it,' he said. Anthony went back to school by train.

My own relationship with Neville was also, on occasion, tempestuous. We had many a blistering row but, looking back, I can recall only a few with any substance. Invariably it was a misplayed hand at bridge that would start us off or, more seriously as the years went by, Neville's urge to eat and drink more than any doctor thought good for him.

Even Neville's affairs, which, of course, were hurtful to me, never made us enemies. I knew what he was like when I married him and knew also that I could not hope to contain the ebullient personality of the old charmer.

When his reputation did catch up with him, it turned out more than anything to be a subject of amusement. A Sunday paper accused him of fathering an illegitimate child. It was a story of the First World War, which Neville denied then and now denied again, though not entirely convincingly since money had changed hands. I was told later that, when Norman had heard the story, he had fallen about laughing: 'Neville was just unlucky. She could have brought a paternity order against any one of a dozen of us!' Still, in the circumstances, Neville's sanctimonious reaction to Anthony's confession of misdeed was, I thought, a little inappropriate.

Soon after the marriage we decided on a move. Saint Hill was rented, and we wanted somewhere to own and to develop. Neville had a hunch that agriculture was to become a lead industry and was keen to invest. We found the ideal property just a few miles from East Grinstead. It was a 300-acre farm flanked by a Tudor-style house, part original, but mostly turn-of-the-century imitation. The view across the open fields was breathtaking: there was not another building in sight.

The asking price for Gotwick Manor was modest, but with some justification. The place was a mess. Military occupation had taken its toll even on the central staircase which, we discovered, had mysteriously disappeared. 'I'm sure it will turn up,' said the agent hopefully, as if it were just the sort of household utility likely to have been borrowed by a neighbour. I need hardly add that his optimism was misplaced.

The farm cottages were in an equally bad way, though here neglect was compounded by the absence of ordinary services. One of the priorities was to bring gas and electricity to the outgoing parts of the estate.

Our association with Gotwick did not start well. On the way to our first viewing Neville misjudged the camber on an unfamiliar road and overturned the car. We climbed out more or less unhurt, but a bit dazed. I sat on the grass verge while Neville wobbled off to get help. By the time a friendly driver had given us a lift back to Saint Hill I felt much better. But this did not deter Miriam Marks, who happened to be calling, from practising her expertise as a Red Cross nurse. We were prescribed gallons of lukewarm tea and ordered to rest, which was the last thing I felt like doing.

When, eventually, we did get to see Gotwick, Neville was full of enthusiasm.

'But what about the cost of renovation,' I protested, trying for a note of realism. 'It'll take a fortune to put this place to rights.'

'Don't worry,' boomed Neville in his grandest manner, 'we can handle it.'

By 'we', I soon found out he meant us and the Ministry of Agriculture. The grants for land development were really quite generous and enabled us to put the estate in working order without losing our shirt.

The Saint Hill staff moved *en masse* to Gotwick. Ripley, who now performed some of the duties of an estate manager, took on an even grander air, if that was possible. Under his charge was Gibbons, the second butler, a cook, a kitchen-maid and a lady's-maid, Miss Emery, whose compulsive neatness extended to stern admonitions to everyone else in the house 'not to touch anything'.

We took possession of Gotwick Manor on VE Day. Among the first visitors was Chaim Weizmann, who brought with him his young secretary. This was the first time I had met George Weidenfeld, though I was to see more of him in the early 1950s when, for a period, he was married to Teddy Sieff's daughter, Jane.

Neville adapted to the life of a gentleman farmer with his customary determination to do everything at once. He joined the East Grinstead and Three Counties Agricultural and Ploughing Association, the County Gentleman's Association whose hard-sell mailings (large stocks – quick delivery – better discounts) belied their genteel image, and the East Grinstead Horse and Cattle Show Society (annual subscription two guineas). Contributions

117

were made to the Vicar's Stipend Fund and to the East Grinstead and District Band, who promptly elected Neville vice-president (non-playing). From a scrap of paper which for years has lined a desk drawer, I discovered that Neville attended at least one District Band committee meeting to discuss earnestly the reconditioning of an E flat tenor horn and the proposed overhaul of a troublesome euphonium.

Neville's farming ambitions centred on the breeding of a superior beef bull, in preparation for which he embarked on a lengthy correspondence course. His dedication was quite unnerving. The return for his efforts was handsome array of show cups and a pile of bills. It seemed impossible to achieve anything in the country without losing money. It was almost a state of mind. To some extent the losses could be offset against other, profitable investments, but only to some extent. Even with ministry grants, and a plethora of advice on how to spend them, in most years we barely made enough to cover wages and feed. When outgoings went two-thirds above income, I thought it was time to call a halt. Fortunately, by then, Neville had other matters to occupy him.

Continuity between Saint Hill and Gotwick Manor was provided by the Queen Victoria Hospital, where I was still an active fund-raiser, mostly on behalf of the new children's wing. Then there were the annual gatherings of the Guinea Pig Club, and frequent visits from Saint Hill Guinea Pigs and their families who happened to be passing through.

We saw less of Archie McIndoe than we would have liked. After the war he distanced himself from East Grinstead partly for financial reasons – to match income with life-style he had to rebuild his Harley Street practice – but also, I fancy, because the hospital was an unsettling place where memories clouded the present. He even talked of an early retirement, which I put down to chronic overwork. Good gracious, he was not yet fifty. But then we heard about Archie's farm in East Africa.

'I can sit on the terrace and look at Kilimanjaro,' he announced proudly.

'Wonderful,' I said but, feeling cynical, added, 'Not really the place for weekends.'

He had a partner, a pilot he had met at East Grinstead, who devoted himself full time to estate management. Archie went out for three months every year. The farm prospered on a full harvest of pyrethrum which, I was given to understand, was vital to the production of insecticides. Maybe we should have tried it at Gotwick.

The plan was for Archie gradually to wind down as a surgeon and to wind up as a farmer. Instead, his life took an unexpected turn: he met Connie.

Their first encounter was in the South of France, where Mrs Constance Belchem, wife of a general, and Sir Archibald McIndoe were on holiday with respective friends. They got on famously, resolving to meet again, though at that point neither knew that the other was in the throes of a marriage break-up.

When their affair became general knowledge, my loyalties were divided. Connie was attractive and amusing; with her Archie rediscovered his zest for life. But until Connie appeared we had all assumed that Archie would eventually marry Jill Mullins, who had kept him going through the war and now shared his home. It was a terrible blow to Jill to find that she was on her own, and a blow to me to realize that Archie could be so brutal.

Even after Archie and Connie were married in 1954, I had to make a conscious effort to like the new Lady McIndoe. But sheer exuberance cannot be resisted for very long. Connie threw herself into Archie's life, loyally supporting him at every turn while handing out good, practical advice. She had to work hard to win over the Guinea Pigs – an exclusive club not given to welcoming outsiders – and succeeded brilliantly. Her annual party for Guinea Pig wives became a high point in the club agenda, a happy antidote to the gung-ho style of military celebration.

And what of Jill? She married a South African businessman. I doubt it was a romance, more a case of settling for a secure, uncluttered life – at a distance. She came home just once more, in 1959. Archie saw her, briefly, and said how much older she looked. She was certainly tired and much quieter than I remembered her. The fun had gone. She went back in September. Two days out, she had a stroke and then another. A few hours before the ship docked at Cape Town, she died.

Neville's wartime stint with the Ministry of Production gave him a taste for politics. Compared to the routine of company management, affairs of state were a thrill a minute, no less so after

Churchill's unexpected defeat in the 1945 election and the advent of a Labour government. Though by no stretch of the imagination a socialist, Neville admired the single-minded dedication of the Labour leaders, from Attlee down, and he enjoyed working for Sir Stafford Cripps, a visionary whose ambitions transcended party barriers.

They had got to know each other in the early part of the war during Cripps's occupancy of the Board of Trade. When in 1942 he switched over to Production, Neville was a natural choice as a go-between for the government and the textile manufacturers. His time was mostly taken up by trying to persuade his erstwhile colleagues in the Lancashire industrial belt to release their workforce into armaments. In this he was quite successful, though he was made to feel the resentment of companies who believed that textiles were being given an unfairly low priority in the national plan.

After the war, instead of returning to Blond Brothers, Neville followed Cripps on his reinstatement to the Board of Trade. Now, as part of the Economic Planning Board, he was expected to reverse the economic thinking of the textile manufacturers – from contraction and penny-pinching to bold expansion. It was all hands to the export drive, with textiles leading the fight for dollar sales.

Neville reacted badly to accusations of inconsistency. War created one set of economic demands, post-war reconstruction quite another. He could not understand the reluctance of his industry to take seriously the need for national planning. He tried to allay fears of a government take-over – at most, he said, Cripps wanted a partnership in which the administration was allowed to speak on behalf of the national interest – and pressed hard for exports to take precedence over the home market. But with scant response. In the first heady months after the victory celebrations, the public expected a release from their long period of self-denial. They wanted a few of the good things in life. Industry did its best to satisfy those demands without regard to the long-term benefit of the economy.

But there was no getting away from the fact that Britain was in bad economic trouble. Having disposed of most of our overseas assets to meet the needs of the military, we had also run up a monstrous debt with the Americans who, paying the compliment of treating us as if we were still a world power, wanted their money back – with substantial interest.

It was only a matter of time before we were caught out in our perverse disregard for economic reality. Meanwhile, Neville and other far-sighted business people, who had no intention of selling out to socialism, railed against industrialists who were so besotted by full order books that they refused to consider investment in new machinery and equipment. 'When they're doing badly,' grumbled Neville, 'they say they can't afford to invest. When they're doing well, they say they don't have to.'

There is a large measure of hindsight coming into all this. At the time, I was not entirely sold on Neville's view of what had to be done to put the country on the road to recovery. With five years of hard graft behind them, the British people deserved a break. Instead, they were being urged to cut back still further on living standards. I understood the need to reconstruct the economic base, but I did wonder if all these government controls – rationing, wage regulations and so on – were the right way of going about it. Some of the ideas mooted for achieving greater efficiency were frankly dotty. One day, Neville came home with a civil-service inspired thought on reducing commuter travelling. 'It's all such a waste,' he explained. 'For instance, there are X thousand people living in Birmingham but working in Coventry and Y thousand people living in Coventry and working in Birmingham. Now you'd think we could organize things better than that.'

'But maybe it's the way they want it,' I suggested. 'Lots of people like living and working in different places. Anyway, what are you going to do about it? Ask them to swop jobs? Or houses? The idea is ridiculous.' But Neville kept worrying at the problem. Such an obviously inept life-style just had to be open to improvement.

I was more in sympathy with Neville's high regard for American business know-how. He was enormously enthusiastic when Cripps set up the Anglo-American Productivity Council and he was closely involved in the Dollar Export Board. He urged anyone with ambition and talent to go to the States (at government expense) to study new manufacturing and marketing techniques.

The American connection was critical for another reason. Vast dollar loans were keeping the British economy afloat, but the terms on which Congress agreed to aid – the free convertibility of sterling into other currencies including the dollar – led to another more serious financial crisis. By mid-1947 the run on the pound had accelerated into full gallop with over £150 million a week leaving the country. Exchange controls were inevitable, but they did not go down well in America where the public saw the British as a weak-kneed lot who were forever crying wolf. Eventually sanity prevailed with the adoption of the Marshall Plan, an economic aid package which applied to all of Western Europe, promoted in a language the Americans understood, to save the old countries from communism.

The immediate pressure was off. At the same time, the need to impress the Americans, to persuade them that we were fulfilling our part of the bargain by pulling ourselves back into economic shape, was more pressing than ever. It was in these circumstances that the idea was mooted of sending a business task-force to America. Its brief was to engage in some energetic flag waving on behalf of British exporters who, as far as anyone could judge, were too modest to do the job for themselves. Neville was canvassed as the leader of this path-blazing project.

In several different ways, he was the ideal choice. A successful industrialist in his own right, Neville had the bluff, outward-going personality best calculated to go down well with straight-talking Americans. He was not part of the upper crust diplomatic service, which turned up its nose at the very mention of commerce. And he was Jewish.

He believed passionately that with more aggressive marketing Britain could win a bigger slice of transatlantic trade. I was not well enough informed to give an opinion. On the other hand, like Neville, I relished a new challenge; and I was not averse to escaping the rule of austerity for a spell. America, with her open and energetic society, was a very inviting prospect.

The idea of making Neville a roving trade ambassador originated with Cripps, but the formal offer came from the young Harold Wilson, who took over at the Board of Trade when Cripps was elevated to the Exchequer. Immediately Neville said yes, we were thrown into a domestic crisis by an instruction to prepare to sail for New York on the last day of July, barely three weeks ahead. What were we going to do about the children?

The boys were both leading independent lives, Anthony at Oxford and Peter in the army. Neither seemed greatly troubled by our extended absence. Ann, too, could fend for herself. Lately out of the Wrens, she was happy to stay in London with her father, who had a flat in Curzon Street, or with Simon and Miriam.

As the youngest, Simone qualified for closer parental attention. She was just back from finishing-school in Switzerland. Why on earth we thought so highly of such places I shall never know. Perhaps it was all part of the desire to break faith with the wartime tradition of hard times and to start work afresh in a happier frame of mind. If this was the objective, with Simone, we failed dismally. She hated the place. On our only visit I began to understand why. With twelve other girls she was lodged in cramped quarters over a garage. The other circumstances of her extended education were equally Spartan. After taking her out for one of the few decent meals she had in Geneva, we decided that Simone had to be a candidate for an extended holiday in America. She jumped at the chance.

An unexpected hitch in these arrangements came when we applied for our American visas. Neville and I were perfectly acceptable, but there was a query over Simone. Why, for heaven's sake? Well, Simone was the daughter of Norman Laski and Norman was the cousin of Harold Laski, the chairman of the Labour Party National Executive Committee and a commie fellow traveller if ever there was one.

Poor Harold. As a university teacher he was a great popularizer of high ideals. But his success with the younger generation led him to overstate his credentials as a practical politician. Though respected in the Labour Party for his intellect, he was also dreaded for his consistency in saying the wrong thing at the wrong time. Attlee could not abide him. Harold's unauthorized avowal, to a conference of French socialists, to expect Britain to move left in its foreign policy, inspired the Prime Minister's classic put down: 'You have no right to speak on behalf of the government . . . a period of silence on your part would be welcome.' After that, Harold was not to be taken seriously.

All of this and more I pointed out to the American immigration officials. I do not believe I told them anything they did not already know, but later I reflected that I may have helped in some small way to put a stop to Harold's ambitions to be appointed an ambassador. I cannot say that I was sorry. The country had enough problems. Anyway, the innocent Simone was cleared.

We sailed on the *Queen Elizabeth* in august company. Sir Oliver Franks, newly appointed ambassador, was on board; so was Foreign Secretary Ernest Bevin. Loyal to my husband's diplomatic credentials, I was politely reserved in my encounters with his political master. Bevin was widely regarded as being anti-Zionist, if not anti-Semitic. Nowadays it is customary to judge his handling of the Palestine issue as an attempt to be even-handed between the Jews and the Arabs. But then, it was all but impossible for us to see him as anything except the apologist of Arab hegemony. Every boatload of Jewish refugees turned away from Haifa was another reason for doubting his understanding of Zionism or its strength of purpose.

I do not believe for one moment that he was malevolent, but he did have a nasty habit of expressing prejudices as facts. His well-timed advice to the Jews to 'wait in line' while he solved other international problems was a clear reflection of the age-old slander that the Jews were too pushy for their own good. A more honest interpretation of recent history might have suggested that the Jews had waited patiently for far too long.

Such was the antipathy between Bevin and the Jewish community, I was vaguely surprised that he had invited a Zionist family to accompany him to the States. I said as much to Sir Oliver Franks, who roared with laughter: 'Don't you see. He needs you for protection. It's his only chance of getting to New York without being lynched.'

There were to be occasions when I began to believe he really meant what he said. According to the American Jews, Britain alone was responsible for the Palestine débâcle. Even Neville and I came in for attack for not doing enough to make our government hand over the Jewish homeland. I had to deliver a few sharp reminders to our hosts that I had been a Zionist before some of them had even heard of the word.

The second surprise of arriving in America was in rediscovering the good life. Everybody complained about shortages, but all I could see were surpluses.

'It's impossible to get meat,' a diplomat's wife told me.

I was annoyed. 'But there's plenty of meat. You can get it at any corner shop.'

'Ah, but not fresh fillets!' Offhand, I could not remember the last time I had seen a fresh fillet.

Our own standard of living in America was variable, to put it mildly. We were not allowed to take very much money with us and while Neville was on generous expenses which covered official engagements including some splendid meals, he was not paid a salary. So, for the first few weeks, until we got our finances in order, we had to content ourselves with window shopping. Simone and I wandered the stores with mounting frustration. The 'new look' – the long, full skirts which, after the uniform years, restored some meaning to the idea of femininity – was not for us. Not yet, anyway.

Also in the first weeks we did a lot of travelling. Neville wanted to visit all the big commercial centres – Chicago, San Francisco, Los Angeles, New Orleans and Toronto – as a first step towards setting up a network of trade embassies. In each of the cities, the resident consul was instructed to look after us. The responsibility was interpreted loosely by those career diplomats who resented Neville's intrusion into their preserve. In Chicago we were left kicking our heels for three days while the British representative fulfilled his 'previous engagements'; in San Francisco a not overworked office staff forgot to book us into a hotel, and in Toronto we were driven into town in a pre-war Hillman which had springs bursting out of the back seat. The hotel, tolerated for one night only, was a dump. It was high summer and there was no air conditioning. For the first and last time in my life, I spent the evening washing out clothes in the sink. Everything shrank.

True to his style, Neville ignored the rebuffs and pressed on with his campaign. The North American market was barely scratched by British exporters. The possibilities were great, but the Americans had to be prepared to give their transatlantic allies a chance to show what they could do. Knowing the power of the media, and enjoying the publicity, he was always at home to a journalist and was prepared to travel all day for the chance of a radio interview. The questioning followed a routine pattern:

'What is it like in Britain; is life as hard as they say it is?'

'Oh yes. Food and clothing are still rationed; petrol is in short supply, but even if you could get it, you might have to wait up to two years to buy a new car. The prices of cigarettes and beer have just gone up by a third.'

'But if it's as bad as that, how can you hope to increase exports?'

'It's because we're holding back on home consumption that we can concentrate on building up the export trade. Already the value of exports is 200 per cent up on the pre-war level. And there's still a long way to go yet.'

There followed a random list of products for which the Americans had a declared liking – from canned herrings to Argyle socks – and an appeal from Neville to put British goods at the top of the shopping list.

He was always on the look-out for opportunities to do deals. One morning over breakfast he read a newspaper report on floods in Oregon. Huge quantities of cement were needed to seal a burst dam. 'Cement,' he mused, 'Now where would we get a few hundred tons of cement?'

'How on earth should I know?'

By lunch he had put through several calls to London. By dinner he had confirmation from the Board of Trade that cargoes of cement afloat somewhere in the Pacific had been diverted to the West Coast. In this way, Neville sold Portland in Dorset to Portland in Oregon, an exercise in twinning which boosted dollar earnings to the tune of $800,000.

Neville impressed even the Americans with his disregard for red tape. The telephone was his favourite short-cut. While others were writing memos, Neville was charming his way down the wires to the person who could give an immediate decision. When a British manufacturer of garden tools sought advice on the sale of a cheap and practical lawn-mower, Neville closed the conversation with a telephone call to a large American mail-order house. Within five minutes he clinched an order worth $200,000.

His other great talent was for finding solutions by looking at problems in a different way. At a Baltimore dinner party, he listened to a deflated businessman who had hoped to set up a patents bureau in London, but the administration had turned down the idea because it would have meant the payment of royalties in dollars. Neville asked a few questions about overlapping commercial interests. Later in the evening, he went back to the man with an idea: 'Why don't you combine your Canadian and UK patent operations in a London office? Then you'll have dollar income as well as dollar outgoings.' A week later, the earlier decision was reversed.

With all the wisdom of Marks and Spencer behind me, I concentrated on the fast dollars to be made from retailing. The huge stores known as supermarkets, then a new word to me but one that was entirely apt, were crowded out with good things. But there was, in my view, a depressing sameness in the rows of brand products.

A store owner in Houston challenged me to come up with an idea for a new product: 'We have it all right here,' he declared confidently. I rattled my brain.

'What about plum puddings?' He did not even pause.

'Plum puddings. Row F, seventh tier.'

'English plum puddings?'

'Ah.' He stalled, not quite knowing if there was any difference between American and English plum puddings. I did not know either, but having started this ridiculous conversation I had to go on.

'More plums in the English variety,' I assured him. 'And a much richer taste. It has something to do with the old country recipe.'

The store owner's enthusiasm mounted: 'You mean, they're *original* English plum puddings?'

He was already hooked on the promotion. Neville had only to put him in touch with a caterer for the sale to be confirmed. I sometimes wonder if you can still buy an English plum pudding in Texas.

Neville's tendency to bypass the official channels did not endear him to the mandarins in Washington. After the welcoming courtesies, which took all of a month, the diplomatic air became too rarefied for comfort. We decided to move to a more accommodating environment. 'New York', said Neville, 'is the only place to be.' I had no reason to disagree with him.

I adored New York. It was open, exciting and forever unexpected. The people were fun and alive with ideas. All things were possible. The glorious informality of the city was revealed to me a day or two after we settled into the Drake Hotel between Park Avenue and Fifth Avenue. Neville asked me where I wanted to go for lunch.

'I don't know. Let's take a stroll; we might find somewhere interesting.'

Out on the street, I caught sight of what looked to be a crowded restaurant – except that there were no waiters or waitresses.

'It's self-service,' said Neville. 'An automat.'

'What's an automat?'

127

'You collect your meal from one of those little cubby-holes along the bar. Just open the door and the meal is waiting for you.'

'Right. That's where we'll have lunch.'

The other customers were a bit surprised to find a woman draped in an expensive fur joining their queue, but not half as surprised as the girl in the kitchen when I talked to her through one of the cubicles. She was putting plates of salad in while I was taking one out.

'It's my first time', I said, 'in an automat. Isn't it a marvellous idea?'

I think it was the accent as much as the admission of appalling innocence which left her open-mouthed for a moment. But she recovered quickly: 'Do you want to take a look? Come on round.' So there we were, on a guided tour of an automat. It was a relaxed, friendly and, in more than one sense, a warming experience. I felt very much at home.

We made many good friends in New York, people who were lively, unusual and exciting – like Melony Kahane, a designer of great talent who later was to have a hand in planning the layout of the space capsule, and her husband Ben Grauer, who started the Voice of America.

Of the British career diplomats my favourite was Frank Evans. An Ulsterman, he was the very model of a Foreign Office high-flyer – tall, grey-haired, urbane and infinitely patient and considerate, qualities which were to come in handy some time later when he was appointed ambassador to Israel. As Consul General, he and Neville saw much of each other. Neville used Frank as a morale booster, a never failing source of good-humoured encouragement when all around was gloom and despair.

At one of their meetings, Frank suggested a lengthy session of Any Other Business.

'Why?' demanded Neville. 'I've another appointment in half an hour.'

'Because,' said Frank, 'in the great American tradition, the building is surrounded. On one side the Jews are protesting about British policy in Palestine, on the other side the Irish are up in arms about British policy in Northern Ireland. That takes care of both of us, don't you think?'

They debated the possibility of an ethnic exchange, Neville tackling the Irish while Frank did his best with the Jews. But by then, drinks had been served and the siege mentality had taken over.

Neville's office was on the sixty-second floor of the Empire State Building. A sedate Humber Imperial was put at our disposal, but it never came out from under its wraps. We travelled everywhere in town by taxi and out of town by train or plane. Neville was one of the first to fly direct from Chicago to Los Angeles. He spent a lot of time on the West Coast, largely, he said, because British business ignored the opportunities there. Later I concluded that there were one or two unofficial attractions in California. Still, there was no denying the apparent inability of British manufacturers to recognize a world beyond New England.

The reluctance to adapt to the needs of the wider market stood out most obviously in the British disregard for colour. Everything we sold was in black, dark blue or brown. Why? A legacy of the war, no doubt, but one we were under no obligation to accept. On the West Coast, where bright colours prevailed, a Lancashire suit or a Midlands motor car (yes, in those days, we really did sell cars to the States!) were said to be too depressing for words.

Commercial insularity was a recurring complaint in Neville's dealings with diplomats and business people. How was it that winning an order for a fleet of London taxis, the manufacturer could respond with a flat refusal to put in left-hand drives? Apparently, the adaptation of the production line was too much trouble for a single order. But why should it be a single order? asked Neville. Once the principle of a sprat to catch a mackerel, British-made cabs might soon be honking all the way across urban America.

When it came to trading with the States, companies which liked to think of themselves as front runners were more interested in what Neville called 'peddling' than in real business. The response from smaller manufacturers was far more encouraging. It was with products like shoes, toys, wallpaper, surgical instruments, biscuits and chocolate that best progress was made. A willingness to take risks was happily combined with a regard for quality, a characteristic not always apparent in companies with famous names.

To prove what could be done, Neville was apt to take an example from what was then the most conservative business of all. The old-established publisher B.T. Batsford surprised everyone, including themselves, with the success of their New York office.

Within a year of setting up, they were operating a clearing-house and marketing service on behalf of some thirty British publishers, including Collins, Methuen and Cassell. It was a great boost to the fortunes of British writers in the United States.

Simone spent her eighteenth birthday in New York. We threw a great party in the Starlight Room of the St Regis Hotel. Simone was delighted with it all, though I fancy, as a war child, she was a little overwhelmed by the extravagance. Her 'new look' costume – a bright green and emerald gaberdine suit – bought specially for the occasion, she kept for years afterwards.

There were many other fabulous parties. In New York, the place to be was the 21 Club, where the charming and affable Burns brothers – Charles and Jerry – dispensed alcoholic euphoria at outrageous prices. One way or another we must have put quite a lot their way, because on our final leave-taking they gave a party for us, an evening of star turns all outclassed by Sophie Tucker, who put in an appearance dressed in a grass skirt, a little number she wore in her show at the Latin Quarter. The talk, what little could be heard, was entirely inconsequential; though I do remember being told, confidentially but on impeccable authority, that Marilyn Monroe and Joe DiMaggio were getting together again.

Away from New York the party of cherished memory was in New Jersey, where Neville was deputized to launch an exciting new drink called Pimm's No.1. Unfortunately, nobody explained that it had to be diluted with lemonade, with the result that guests knocked back neat Pimm's as if it were Coca-Cola. Afterwards, those capable of assessing its appeal suggested it should best be promoted not as pick-me-up but more as a put-me-down.

When Peter and Anthony came over on a visit, the whole family took off for California. The main draw was the glamour of Hollywood, which we managed to compress into an exhausting and, I would have thought, exhaustive tour of the studios. The climax was a great custard-pies battle, fought out on an Abbott and Costello set. Inevitably a hit-and-miss affair – whenever there was a miss you could be sure the director wanted a hit and vice versa – the event was, for me, more fun off-screen than on. I came to think that film comedy might have more to offer if mistakes were left in.

Peter did not waste any time. He collected a load of telephone numbers which he used to good effect back in London. When I tried to reach him one day I was told he was at lunch with a young actress called Elizabeth Taylor.

The family link with California was through my uncle Barnet, who had also gone into store-keeping, if on a more modest scale. He was still alive and well, though no longer active in business. He had a daughter, two years older than myself, and two sons, one of whom, Josh, was an architect who built the Santa Fe racecourse. I much admired this piece of handiwork and told him that he had grossly undercharged for his efforts. The thought had already occurred to him and representation to the governing committee had been made. But instead of a supplement to his fee, he was paid off with a life membership. I am inclined now to believe he got the best of the deal after all.

I cannot say that family affairs went too well in California. With the best of intentions I gave a reception for all those relatives and friends who, in the war, had helped out with gifts of clothes and food for our refugee children. But I was faced with a boycott. No one wanted to come, it was said, because as a diplomat's wife, albeit of temporary status, I was associated with British government intransigence in Palestine. I was at first angry, but then enormously depressed.

It was after this experience, though not because of it, that I decided I had had enough of the American high life. It had been a glorious diversion, a perfect holiday, but it was time to go home. The bouts of restlessness were intensified by the suspicion that Neville's attachment to his admittedly attractive secretary went beyond diplomatic propriety. When the suspicion became a certainty, I called a halt.

My demand for a home posting, put to Neville in terms which invited a row, was received much to my surprise almost enthusiastically. He too felt it was time for a change. With trade offices now established in nearly all the leading cities, it was natural that the pioneering excitement of Neville's work should diminish. But his dissatisfaction arose more from the constant sniping of business people who resented his badge of officialdom and made clear that they could do very well without the help of Mr Blond, thank you. We came back to London in mid-December 1949. One of our last official duties was to accompany Harold Wilson on a visit to Chicago. There, Neville was presented with what he thought was a wonderful opportunity to go out on a high note. Talks with a big mail-order firm led to a provisional order for five million Sheffield hunting knives. There was delight all round. Neville gave a press conference at which the President of the Board of Trade undertook to arrange for this export prize to be shared out since no single company could fulfil the order within the specified time.

Back in New York and in the chaos of packing, Neville was handed an urgent cable from Whitehall asking for more details of the surprisingly large order. It appeared that no one in London, or Sheffield for that matter, knew anything about it except what they read in the newspapers. Neville did some telephoning. What was going on? It was all a misunderstanding, a dreadful mistake. The order was not for five million knives. An assessment of the market had revised the likely demand to twenty thousand, maybe only fifteen thousand. The news made for a subdued last evening. Even on the *Queen Mary*, where service and comfort could usually be guaranteed to dispel the darkest mood, Neville was strangely quiet.

I knew how he felt. It may sound vain, but after two years of unpaid public service Neville hoped to be elevated above the OBE he had been awarded after the war. I fully shared his ambition. The last thing we needed was to leave America in the wake of an almighty balls-up. Still, the saga of the knives (raising associations of back-stabbing) had to be seen in perspective. Overall, Neville had scored a notable personal success. Even if the jump in exports to the US (fifteen per cent in a single year) could not be solely attributed to the trade adviser, he had certainly helped more than most to bring it about. To take a leading part in what Harold Wilson described a little clumsily as 'the greatest challenge in the history of the merchant adventuring spirit of the British traders' was surely worthy of recognition.

Two weeks later when we were settling back into Gotwick, a strictly personal call came through for Neville. He went to the telephone in the library. When he came back, he was looking thoughtful.

'What is it?' I asked.

Assuming I was asking a particular rather than a general question, he said, 'The CMG.'

I was mystified.

'The CMG,' he repeated. 'Companion of the Order of St Michael and St George.'

The mist cleared.

'Oh, that's wonderful,' I said. And then I thought – 'Companion', not 'Knight'. It was just a CMG.

We both sat and looked at each other. I thought, 'Poor Neville,' but he said it out loud, 'Poor Elaine.'

Family Affairs

In May 1948 we celebrated the creation of the State of Israel. No one deluded themselves that it was the end of the struggle; rather that it was a new beginning.

We expected war. The outright rejection by the Arabs of the United Nations partition of Palestine made it all but inevitable. A taster of what was to come was provided by the Egyptian reaction to the news of the birth of Israel: planes were sent to drop bombs on Tel Aviv.

We arrived home from America while the War of Independence was at its height. For the Marks, as for other Jewish families, it was the greatest political event in our lives. Even those who were not in the least Zionist could not help but be swept along on the wave of Jewish chauvinism.

As the leader of British Jewry, Simon was active behind the scenes, attending one meeting after another and keeping up a flow of correspondence to political leaders soliciting help for the cause. By contrast, sister Becky actively sought the limelight. Her highpoint of Zionist exhibitionism was a mile-long procession of determined ladies, which she led from the Mansion House to a rally in Trafalgar Square. Her call to action, echoing from the loudspeakers across the massed audience, is remembered to this day as a stunning affirmation that all things were possible.

But Becky was unsettled. She was convinced that she could do more good in Israel and was not happy until she had persuaded her WIZO colleagues to move their headquarters, lock, stock and barrel, to Tel Aviv. She was probably right. The burgeoning of WIZO responsibilities – the population of Israel doubled in less than two years – made a nonsense of trying to direct affairs from London.

In Israel, she had built a splendid two-storey villa with terraced gardens, a fountain and a pool, at Tel Mond, close to the Arab border. From there she directed the WIZO endeavour to bring health, education and other welfare services to the poor and often deprived immigrants who were pouring into the community at a rate of ten thousand a month.

The departure of WIZO from Britain left the FWZ as the body chiefly responsible for making available the resources demanded by Becky. Into this work I plunged as, first, joint chairman of fund-raising, then as chairman of finance and vice-chairman of the whole organization. I also took on the chair of the West London Women's Zionist Society. This side of my life reminded me always of my days at school when my sisters had been held up as the paragons, whose standards I could not even hope to emulate. While Becky forged away in Israel, the driving force in London was sister Miriam. It was she who persuaded the FWZ to shoulder responsibility for particular projects – a kindergarten, say, or a children's clinic. In this way, people giving money could see how it was being spent and, naturally, as a consequence, gave yet more.

The biggest single adoption of the FWZ was the Jerusalem Baby Home, which had been set up in the 1920s to rescue abandoned and neglected infants. Those were the days when charity began with improvisation: the cots were made out of old orange boxes. Always overcrowded to the point of bursting, the Baby Home could not cope with all the child casualties of the immigrant shanty towns around Jerusalem. Deciding that nothing less than a new building would do, Miriam, with Tilly in support, bought land on a hillside in Beth Hakerem. Building was interrupted by the War of Independence, but resumed in late 1948 with an appeal for $250,000 to finish the job. The FWZ asked for five years to raise the entire sum. (Remember this was pre-1950 when the pound, as they used to say, was worth a pound.) We hit the target one year ahead of schedule.

Though there was less money around in those days, the fight for survival in Israel was a spur to generosity. It was always the same when the country was in crisis. What was more of a challenge was to keep the money rolling in when Israel was out of the headlines. The other problem was trying to explain that we were not seeking just minimum standards in health and education or simply trying to fill the gaps left by the state. In our areas of special concern – mostly support for needy mothers and children – we set our sights on achieving the best. As Becky was forever reminding us, if Israel was to survive, the quality of life there had to be more than tolerable; it had to be an ideal to which others could aspire.

The FWZ had its own problem of standards. The accumulation of work was too much for the old administration, cramped into its store-cupboard offices in Great Russell Street. It was time for a move. But the FWZ could not be seen to be spending hard-won donations on equipping itself with fancy new premises. Miriam had the answer. She simply bought a handsome Regency house in Gloucester Place and handed it over as a gift. When, a few years later, yet more space was needed, she went shopping again for the house next door. No wonder she was known as the fairy godmother of the FWZ.

All the sisters had our pet projects in Israel for which we provided all, or the bulk, of the finance. Mine were the Blond Day Care Centre in Tel Aviv, the Burns Unit at the Rambam Hospital in Haifa and the Arab Children's Theatre at the Omariya School in East Jerusalem. This last was as open a declaration as I could make of my belief in positive coexistence with the Arabs. It is not good enough to argue that in creating the outpost of civilization in the Middle East, the Jews deserved to keep the best for themselves. I regret more has not been done to win the understanding of the Arabs living in Israel and to harness their ability and energy for the common cause. The popularity of the Children's Theatre and its impact on other community projects involving Arab children gives a hint of what can be achieved.

The Burns Unit was still under construction when the Yom Kippur War broke out in October 1973. Formally opened a month later, it was already fully occupied by casualties. The doctors, most of whom had been trained at East Grinstead, barely had time to acknowledge the official recognition of their existence. I was proud of the Burns Unit, but impatient with Israeli bureaucracy which had a dictatorial view on how money should be spent. After one visit when I found the paint peeling off the walls ('Unattractive and unhygenic,' I told the administrator), I offered to pay for a complete redecoration. The money was accepted quickly enough, but when I returned a few months later, conditions had deteriorated still further. 'Why?' I demanded to know. It was simple, really. The rules did not allow for renovation until all demands for medical equipment had been budgeted. But this, I pointed out, postponed the redecoration indefinitely. Doctors would always want new equipment. It was in their nature. Would I have to wait for the Burns Unit to start falling down before I could dispose of my money as I wanted? Since the question was not answered, I drew my own conclusions.

I went to Israel two or three times a year, but in London the FWZ occupied two or three days a week. My secretary, Betty Goldstein, a huge motherly woman who kept a tight hold on my social and business affairs, made a regular point of telling me that I did too much: 'They ring you up for every little thing. Why don't you tell them to make up their own minds?' She was quite capable of turning visitors away from the door if she thought their call was unnecessary. Such was her force of personality, not to mention her physical presence, that few of her victims ever appealed against a decision.

But I had no need to be protected from the FWZ. I loved the work which gave me and gave us all a wonderful sense of fulfilment. There were times when I lost patience – usually with those who told me that we were running ahead of ourselves. If an area council complained that its financial quota was too high, I was armed with a battery of statistics to show how much more money was raised by WIZO in Israel. 'Not only do they do the work, but they bring in over half the budget!' Was not this, I argued, a cause for shame?

To add force to any speech from me on the subject, I wheeled on a succession of eminent people who, at one time, had themselves been immigrants, in need of a friendly hand from WIZO. At Leeds, when there was some little local difficulty, I persuaded Joan Comay, wife of the Israeli ambassador, to join me on the platform. She told of her arrival in Israel, a young girl in a boat packed with internees lately released from a Cypriot camp. She was nervous and uncertain. Then, as the boat anchored, she recognized a WIZO greeting – a Sabbath table spread the full length of the Haifa dock – and, immediately, she felt at home. After hearing that story, it was a long time before Leeds failed to meet its quota.

Even my West London branch, which I confess often did take up more hours than could be justified by results, had its moments. One of the duties taken on by WIZO was to help immigrants, often from European or Oriental cities, who found themselves trying to adapt to a pioneering life in Israel's desert outposts. Once there, they were left by the government to fend for themselves. The newspapers called them 'the forgotten people'. Forgotten, that is, by all except WIZO, who gave practical advice and guidance in coping with daily problems.

As a gesture of support, the West London ladies took the brave step of twinning their group with the township of Yeruham, in the far south. I made a visit there and saw the terrible hardships endured by these people. Shelter was primitive, the services non-existent. The midday temperature was 120 in the shade, except, as a friend pointed out, there was no shade. It all seemed a world away from the comfortable homes of West London. Yet there was our day crèche, serving the needs of mothers who had to be out working alongside their husbands. Other services followed, but sadly we could not provide what was most needed – human contact. The people of Yeruham could not escape the conviction that the rest of Israel did not care about them. It is a long time since I visited the town. I hope today they get a better deal.

While we were in America Ann went off with a Marks and Spencer delegation to South Africa. For her, it was a holiday, but for Simon who led the expedition it was a business trip. He never went anywhere unless it was on business.

The link to South Africa was a 12½ per cent interest in a retail chain known as Woolworth. I labour the description because Woolworth South Africa was not the Woolworth we all thought we knew. It was started by Max Sonnenberg, a pioneer trader who recognized the potential value of a well-established name. He might just have probably chosen Marks and Spencer. F. W. Woolworth tried to stop him, but by the time their lawyers got themselves into gear, it was too late. The courts ruled that the thriving business built up by Max under his assumed name could not now be taken away.

Simon and Max were introduced at a time when Simon was looking for opportunities abroad. They liked each other, and a share deal was agreed after which Simon decided he wanted to inspect his investment. He was disappointed. South African retailing fell far short of the Marks and Spencer standard, and there was much hard talk about beefing up the management to give better service.

Ann, meanwhile, was provided with an escort to show her the sights. The son of a Woolworth's director, David Susman was a university student, lately demobbed from the South African army. By all accounts the young people got on moderately well in an impersonal sort of way. There was no question of a relationship, at least not until a year or so later when Ann heard from a friend that

David had gone back to the army – the Israeli one this time – had been wounded in the War of Independence and was recovering in hospital in Johannesburg.

When he went back to Israel it was via London to see Ann. After two days they were engaged. I was surprised. I was even more surprised when they said they were to be married in three weeks. Of course, I told them it was quite impossible. I might as well have been talking to myself.

Off they went to Israel for two years where David, who was among the brightest of his generation, shifted over from the military to the diplomatic corps. Under Teddy Kollek, his boss at the Foreign Ministry, his path to ambassadorial status seemed assured. But, emotionally, it was not easy for Ann and David to come to terms with the prospect of yet another cultural allegiance. Ann was English; David, a South African; both were Israelis by adoption. Now they had to think of resettling – yet again – in Washington. For such young people (they were barely half-way into their twenties) it was all a bit too much.

They decided to come to London for a spell. What I thought was a skilfully diplomatic message went to Simon asking his advice on the proposed move. He was not taken in.

'They didn't ask me about going to Israel,' he told me, 'so why should they ask me about coming to London?'

'Because he needs a job,' I said. 'I should think that's obvious.'

'Of course he needs a job. I know that. So why doesn't he say so?'

Taking the hint, David revised his tactics, putting a direct question to Simon. But still the patriarch held out – until the young man's patience was exhausted. 'If you don't want me at Marks and Spencer', he declared, 'I'll go elsewhere.' *Then* Simon offered him a job.

I heartily approved, but in a short while I was regretting my first enthusiasm. From the start, I suspect, Simon had his eye on David as a likely saviour of Woolworth's South Africa. He was too smart to approach the subject directly. Instead, after David had found his feet in the retail trade, he made threatening noises about the Marks and Spencer investment in South Africa.

'The company is in a mess,' he declared. 'I don't know why we bother. Perhaps it's time to sell up.'

David rose to the bait: 'You keep sending the wrong people. You need someone who is young, energetic, imaginative.'

'Precisely,' said Simon.

After that, David could not very well refuse the job.

Ann was less easily persuaded. So was I. But Simon got his way on the promise that it would not be for ever. 'It needs a year or two at most,' he prophesied. Five years later when Ann was in London on holiday we went to tackle Simon in his office. I played the angry mother while Ann piled on the sentiment, even at one stage bursting into tears.

'But what's wrong with South Africa?' Simon demanded to know.

'It's so cut off,' blubbed Ann.

'Cut off? Cut off from what?'

'From everything that's going on here.'

Simon shouted for his secretary: 'Mrs Susman feels cut off. Arrange for her to get the *Illustrated London News*.'

A copy arrived the following week and subsequent issues have been turning up at monthly intervals ever since. Twenty years on, Ann and David are still in South Africa, though with David's appointment to the main Marks and Spencer board, they spend almost as much time in London as they do in the Cape.

While possibly worrying too much about Ann, I certainly worried too little about Simone. She had grown up to be an attractive and, I thought, a self-assured young lady. I admired her pluck when, after starting on the ground floor of Marks and Spencer, she took up fashion modelling, a tough business by any standards. Simon was appalled, though I am still not sure what it had to do with him. Simone, to her great credit, refused to be bullied and went her own way.

In 1952 she married a handsome young doctor called Al Caplan. I was enormously taken with Al. He was witty, charming and entertaining, but there was a sort of helplessness about him. A mutual friend said of Al that he needed looking after. I thought I understood though, in fact, it was two years before I realized quite how much looking after he required. Simone discovered the truth less than twenty-four hours after signing the register: Al was homosexual.

At a time when homosexuality was still taboo, it is possible that he saw marriage as a cure, or at least a counterbalance to his problem. Even now, I find it difficult to believe that his motives for the relationship were entirely cynical. But the rate at which he got through Simone's money suggests otherwise. Abandoning medicine as too humdrum an occupation, he turned to the theatre as a mode of self-expression. It was an expensive diversion. A single show like *Jubilee Girl*, which came and went at the Lyric, Hammersmith, lost a fortune. Its sole kudos was to launch the career of Fenella Fielding.

A happier venture was an investment in *Cranks*, a dance review created by John Cranko, the choreographer who later directed the Stuttgart Ballet. But while the critics were kind and audiences enthusiastic, the box office failed to turn in a profit, at least for Simone.

Al, meanwhile, collaborated on several musicals which no one wanted to see or listen to. He and Simone still lived in the same house, but barely spoke to each other. Of course, I knew there was tension, but until the last dreadful scene in the charade, I had no idea of the misery Simone had had to endure. Why not? Simone was convinced that I would not understand. Probably she was right. I was of a generation which still had much to learn of adult relationships. When the lessons were too painful I, like many others, was quick to put the defences. It is some comfort to know that Simone was able to talk to Archie McIndoe.

The crunch came when Al's boyfriend moved in. Simone moved out. It took her three years to get the divorce and about the same time to clear the backlog of debts. By then Al was on the drugs which were eventually to kill him. To the end he was desperately seeking assurance that his was not a wasted life, but no one could give him that.

Simone's story, I am delighted to say, had a much happier progression. When she married again it was to a young solicitor who was active in London politics. Tony Prendergast had many qualities but, as I could not help pointing out, he was deficient in one respect. Nothing serious; anyway, not from my point of view, but there were those who might be a little surprised to observe that, not to put too fine a point on it, Tony was not Jewish.

We worried a lot about who was to break the news to Simon. In the end, it was Simone who decided that she alone would face the onslaught. The encounter was a total anticlimax. Simon appeared unconcerned by this radical departure from tradition. Only when Simone was leaving did he give something approaching a reason for his forbearance. 'Our family', he told her, 'has been so busy behaving as Zionists, we've forgotten our religion.'

Like everyone else in the family, Simone came to a point where she decided never to leave another moment of her life unoccupied. Without naming all the organizations in which she became a leading figure (I am not even sure I can remember the exhaustive list), I can say that her undertakings range from the magistrates bench to the resettlement of refugees. She richly deserved the OBE she was awarded in 1981, a double honour as it turned out because in the same year, Tony, a former Lord Mayor of Westminster, got the CBE.

Of my two stepsons, Anthony continued on the path of outrageousness. After dabbling in this and that he persuaded his father to set him up as a publisher, an occupation which suited his flamboyant nature, if not his incurable extravagance. He was a true child of the anarchic 1960s. He brought out books which offended established views, put money into *Private Eye* and gave mad parties for well-heeled rebels like himself.

Anthony's idea of a party was to go through the telephone directory. No matter what time you arrived there was always a crowd. They came because they knew the occasion would be extraordinary. When he unveiled his home off the Regent Canal, we dug into a thirty-pound iced cake and took our drinks from a fountain flowing with red wine. The building was of a curious design. There were no windows at all on the street side, but one huge studio window looked out over the garden and the water. Because Anthony liked space, he cut out the bedrooms. I was not surprised when, as the party got under way, he announced that he had already decided to sell the place.

Peter tells of the Anthony party which was so crowded that he decided to escape to a local pub for a breather. When we walked in, there at the bar, looking wonderfully relaxed, was his host.

'Might not the guests think this a little impolite?' suggested Peter.

'You're quite right,' said Anthony, 'You'd better go back.'

As a publisher, Anthony had a knack for spotting winners. Simon Raven was one of his finds, and Anthony was the first in the UK to exploit the mass appeal of Harold Robbins. In education, which in those days was topsy-turvy with new ideas, he produced books which were interesting and informative, an achievement which alone deserved an award for community service.

But he was a mass of inconsistencies. A Labour candidate in 1963, he had turned Liberal by the next election. As with politics, so with people. He could never make up his mind. He had girlfriends and boyfriends. His son, whose appearance upset Neville so much, was born to a lady with a passion for variety. According to Anthony, she had four other illegitimate children, all by different fathers – an electrical engineer, a gypsy, a short-story writer and a Chinese-Indian folk singer. She professed to be a strict Roman Catholic.

He will hate me for saying it, but Anthony has of late shown distinct signs of settling down. His charming wife, Laura, younger but much steadier than he, has achieved wonders. But I would not want to bet against a few more surprises before his time is up.

As the quieter brother, Peter as a young man was overwhelmed by Neville, who did not expect him to succeed. But in the curious way in which family assumptions can go a long way towards achieving the opposite, Peter set out to prove himself an astute and imaginative businessman.

After working for a time at Blond Brothers he raised a loan of £5,000 to buy himself a disused cinema in Wigan. He then converted this unlikely purchase into a factory and started making blouses for Marks and Spencer. Today he has a full design team, four factories turning out a range of women's clothes, and some of the most advanced manufacturing processes anywhere in the country. It is a virtue which counts for a lot with his quality-conscious customer in Baker Street.

My worries about Peter centred on his passion for motor racing. As a young man, he was mad about cars. Neville promised to buy a runabout as a twenty-first birthday present as long as he kept off smoking and drinking before that date. Peter stuck to the bargain much to our surprise. Neville asked Anthony what he thought his brother would do if for some reason he did not get his car. Anthony had no doubts: 'He'll kill himself.'

This is what I thought he was trying to do when he borrowed some money from David Susman to buy a racing model. But he did well on the big circuits including Le Mans and the Nuremberg Ring without breaking any limbs. Several of his friends were not so lucky, and I am sure that Peter himself realized there was a limit to the number of times he could expect to walk away unharmed from a smoking pile of scrap metal. Thankfully, in 1960, he exchanged motor racing for marriage, the best bargain of his life.

Peter got much closer to his father in later life. His wife, Virginia, ever patient, did much to win Neville round. He even gave up calling her Veronica, which he did for years, said Peter, just to be difficult. Their daughter, Rebecca, started dancing classes at about the time when Neville went into hospital. When Peter visited him, Neville wanted to know how Rebecca was getting on.

'Not very well,' said Peter.

'Why not?'

'She refuses to dance.'

'I see.'

'And there's worse.'

'What could be worse?'

'When Madame tried to persuade her, Rebecca told her to "piss off".'

The laughter, Peter told me, could be heard the full length of the corridor. Neville loved the thought of the old spirit coming out in his grandchild. Especially as he now knew it was there in plenty in both his sons.

Blond-McIndoe

Boxing Day 1958 began like every other Boxing Day I can remember, as a day of recovery. I had breakfast in my room, emerging after a few rejuvenating cups of coffee to find Neville wandering about in an aimless sort of way, searching, he said, for some papers he had left out the evening before and which had now mysteriously disappeared. Both still in our dressing-gowns we retreated to the morning-room to relax with the Christmas selection of light novels.

Ripley came in: 'There is a visitor, Madam.'

Since no member of the family would have required a formal announcement, and we were not expecting anyone else, we went into the 'guess who' routine which Ripley took to be the proper way for a butler to get to the point.

'Anyone we know?' asked Neville.

'I don't believe so, Sir. But you may know *of* him.'

'Well?' The note of impatience was not lost on Ripley.

'Mr Watson, Sir. From the Queen Victoria Hospital.'

'At this time in the morning. It must be something serious.'

It was. But not quite in the manner we expected.

John Watson was one of the new generation of plastic surgeons. Demobbed in 1947, a trained and by now highly experienced surgeon, he started in his more specialist line of medicine by persuading Archie to take him on. They had first met in the operating theatre at East Grinstead. When John arrived at what seemed to him to be an unnecessarily early hour, Archie was already hard at work. 'He had on a white coat,' John remembered. 'At least it was white from the back. The front was covered in blood.' The usual introductions were quickly bypassed. 'Can you mend a watch?' Archie demanded. John said yes, he thought he could. And that was the only conversation which passed between them while sundry patients were wheeled in and out. Eventually, Archie spoke again. 'Can you start tomorrow?' Again John said, yes, he could. He was never told which weighed heaviest in his appointment – availability, patience or his skill (untested) as a watch repairer.

John became the first to be awarded a Marks Fellowship in Plastic Surgery. As a McIndoe protégé, he was one of the group of visionaries who looked to the war years at East Grinstead as just the start of far-reaching changes in applied surgery. They had already come a long way. The departments of plastic, oral and corneo-plastic surgery, the latter under Sir Benjamin Rycroft, a wartime colleague of Archie's, were world famous. A successful campaign to liberalize the law on the transfer of tissues and organs from the dead to the living had opened up the prospect of a huge expansion of transplantation surgery.

But before that could happen there was a biological brain teaser to solve. The challenge was to find ways of adapting the body's immune system to ensure that transplanted tissues and organs would not be rejected by the host body. So far this could only be achieved in corneal grafting. Other transplants, except in the case of identical twins, usually died after a few weeks – long enough only for skin grafts where the patient was given the respite he needed to grow his own replacement tissue.

Clearly, if East Grinstead was to continue on its trail-blazing path, a research unit was needed. The concept attracted Russell Davies, Archie's chief anaesthetist and, like John, a natural organizer. Together, they did a few costings: £10,000 was needed to put up and equip a building. Would we, asked John, be willing to contribute?

I was immediately excited by the idea; likewise Neville. To solve the problem of tissue rejection had to be one of the noblest aims of medical science. It was entirely fitting that East Grinstead should have its chance to work the miracle. Without needing to reflect, Neville and I agreed on the spot to put up the full £10,000.

I think John was a little surprised to get so far so quickly. Long afterwards I discovered that he had neglected to tell Archie he was coming to see me. Probably, he imagined, there was time enough to involve the great man when he had a clearer idea of the likely financial support. Now, after a single meeting, he had enough to cover all but the operational costs. He expected Archie to be a little upset at not being consulted earlier. In the event Archie was more than upset; he was furious. What John had not appreciated was that Archie had his own pet project, the rehabilitation of the Royal College of Surgeons of which he was the vice-president.

With an appeal to raise £2 million well under way, I was high on Archie's list as a prospective subscriber. Now, he feared, John had syphoned off whatever Blond money was available. But he soon came round to the idea. Unwittingly, we may have smoothed the way by confounding his expectations with a substantial gift to the Royal College of Surgeons. But even if we had held back, I am sure Archie would have got all he wanted from the head of the Marks family.

I introduced Simon to the Queen Victoria clan when he was in need of a hernia operation. So well did Archie fulfil his patient's request for a painless experience that Simon immediately put himself at the head of the McIndoe admiration society. The Royal College was among the early beneficiaries. A promise of £52,000 over seven years was topped up by another £100,000 not more than a week after John Watson's visit to Gotwick. The timing was fortuitous, but I have no doubt it put Archie into a happier frame of mind.

The younger surgeons at the Queen Victoria were unanimous in their support for the research unit. For those already engaged in experimental work, any improvement was welcome. Robin Beare, whose makeshift laboratory was the sister's office of a disused ward, led the chorus of approval for John to go out to raise yet more money.

He began with the Leverhulme Trust, which promised £4,000 a year for seven years, to help cover salaries and administrative costs. To quote John on his encounter with Sir Miles Clifford, director of the Trust: 'I asked him for money to support a scientist who had not been appointed to work on a research project which had not been defined in a building which had not been built, and he said "Yes".'

Shortly afterwards Johnson and Johnson, the drug company, made a grant of £3,000 a year, also for seven years. From the Ministry of Health came an allocation of land at the rear of the hospital, close by the plastic surgery unit.

We were doing so well. But then, suddenly, we had cause to wonder if we could go on; if it was worth going on. The blow came on the morning of 13 April 1960. Connie rang and Neville took the call. From his side of the conversation I knew it was bad news. When he put down the phone he told me, quietly, 'Archie died last night.'

That Archie's health had not been of the best, we were all aware. But his problems seemed to be manageable. Towards the end of the war, complaining of stomach pains, he was persuaded to call in a top surgeon who found nothing but an overworked liver. When the pains continued, Archie had another operation. This time the top surgeon did find something – the swab he had left in after his first exploration. Then there was an operation for Dupuytren's Contracture and one to remove cataracts in both eyes. Throughout all this and more, Archie remained unfailingly cheerful. I still have a letter he sent me from hospital written, as he said, 'more or less upside down with my rear end in a perfectly shocking position'. He was to be operated on the following day or, as he put it, 'Tomorrow is D-Day and the Huns move in.' He ended, 'I have learned a good deal of patience in the last few weeks and the antics of my carcase no longer surprise me.'

What he kept from us was the knowledge that his heart was weak. His doctors urged him to slow down, but this he could not do. Forced to cut back on the time he spent in the theatre, he transferred his energies to the Royal College of Surgeons.

The financial appeal, which raised £2 million in less than a year, was a triumph of energetic campaigning. But it put Archie at the centre of a controversy which doubled the strain and took away much of the pleasure of achievement. A forceful group of doctors complained of the barn-storming methods adopted by Archie to attract support for the Royal College. Though barely meriting attention by today's standards, Archie was denigrated for the unseemly use of press and television to promote (it was implied) his own interests. The personal element was Archie's bid for the presidency of the Royal College. There could be no doubt that the appeal was a factor in his election. And why not? What the profession needed most was hard cash. Perhaps, also, they needed someone who was not afraid to ask for it. But for many doctors a mere reference to money constituted ungentlemanly behaviour. The vicious backbiting, which was clearly taking its toll on Archie, was halted by his only opponent for the presidency. With characteristic generosity, Arthur Porritt, now Lord Porritt, stood down to give Archie a free run.

It was thus in a contented frame of mind that Archie attended an official dinner on the evening of 12 April. He was given a lift home by Lord Evans, the Queen's Physician, whom he invited in for a drink. They talked until one in the morning. Archie had great plans for the Royal College, but it was others who would have to bring them to reality.

After the first shock, we at East Grinstead likewise took the realistic view. It was nonsense to believe that because Archie had gone, the research project had to be abandoned. In fact, the argument for pressing on gained force as we realized that here was the chance to enhance the meaning of one man's life. The first official act under the new regime was for the trustees to give a name to their effort. Henceforth, we were to work on behalf of the McIndoe Memorial Research Unit. When the buildings were completed they were named the McIndoe Centre.

The next step was to recruit a team leader, but no obvious candidate presented himself. The trustees naturally insisted on excellence, but they did not want a big name who was past his prime. Rather they looked for a younger man (the chances of finding a woman were non-existent), who showed promise of brilliance. After much canvassing, a name was put forward by Professor Peter Medawar, himself a leading researcher into the power of the human body to discriminate between its own and other living cells.

The scientist we wanted was at the University of Copenhagen. Though barely into his thirties, Dr Morten Simonsen had already made a significant contribution to the science of immunology by showing how, under certain conditions, a graft would attack its host, causing a wasting disease known as G v H (graft versus host). The recommendation came with a warning that Dr Simonsen was, to say the least, an unconventional academic. But, claimed Medawar, there was no doubt he could do the job.

A nomination from one of the best scientific brains in the country (Medawar's discovery that immunological tolerance could be induced in animals by blood injections was to earn him a Nobel Prize) had to be treated seriously.

The trustees voted for negotiations to open, though John Watson was worried about the money. 'He'll be expensive,' he told us.

'Never mind,' said Neville, who was impatient for action. 'We can handle it.'

So, with reservations as to the nature and degree of Dr Simonsen's singularity, John, as secretary to the Trust, was deputized to seek out the Dane and offer him the directorship. There was an immediate difficulty of locating Dr Simonsen. John wrote to him in

Copenhagen, but was told by the university that our quarry was at a conference in Barcelona. When communication with Spain proved inadequate for his purpose, John decided to intercept Dr Simonsen at Heathrow where he was due to change flights on his way home to Denmark.

There was no problem in recognizing the tall, stringy character, dressed like a West Coast hippy, who emerged from customs looking, as John tactfully put it, as if he needed a long rest. They started talking on the escalator. Was Dr Simonsen interested in the East Grinstead job? Possibly. Maybe. There was a prospect of Copenhagen University creating a special laboratory for research into homo transplantation. But at East Grinstead a laboratory was already under construction. Dr Simonsen agreed to come and see, to meet the people involved. He and John drove direct from the airport. The slow, jolting excursion around London did nothing to improve the spirits of the prospective head of research. He started the journey looking the worse for wear and ended it in urgent need of medication. Dr Simonsen made his own diagnosis and suggested a remedy: a large whisky. This he drank and promptly collapsed. It was not a good start.

When he recovered from what turned out to be a severe attack of dysentery, Dr Simonsen quickly persuaded his peers that he was all that Peter Medawar had promised.

But agreeing terms was not an easy matter. The prospective director did not underestimate his own worth, nor was he inhibited in his criticisms of the building as planned. He wanted more space, more equipment and more staff. To meet some of his demands and to cover the inevitable underestimate on the overall cost, Neville and I put in another £10,000 and a contribution towards running expenses.

A deal was struck, though, with half an eye on Copenhagen where the university was promising a bigger and better laboratory some day, Dr Simonsen signed on for only two years. While this was too short a time for solid achievement, the consensus held that if conditions were promising the new director would stay longer. The consensus was right. Morten Simonsen was at East Grinstead for six years, long enough to fulfil Neville's prophecy. 'That man', he said after their first encounter, 'will put the McIndoe Centre on the map.'

We opened in March 1961. Enoch Powell, then Minister of Health, gave an official blessing, consisting of a speech in praise of voluntary effort. 'It will be a poor day for medicine,' he concluded, 'if medical research has to be controlled by a ministry.' After that, we were on our own.

Morten Simonsen turned out to be a prodigious worker, a man not easily deflected from his chosen course. He held uncompromising left-wing views (as we discovered when MI5 came to visit), which may have accounted for his lack of inhibition in manipulating the capitalist system for all it was worth.

As chairman of the trustees, Neville was often called upon to intercede when demands from the director's office outreached the trustees' capacity to deliver. There was the occasion when the employment of another brilliant young immunologist became a matter of pressing urgency. No problem, except that the gentleman in question, Dr Hilliard Festenstein, just happened to be in Johannesburg – in prison. He was in detention under the ninety-day rule which sanctioned the arbitrary arrest of political agitators. But could he get out? The word from South Africa was of his release within a week. Subsequently, he and his family were booked on a flight to London. The day came and so did the scientist's wife and children, but of Dr Festenstein there was no sign. Urgent enquiries at South Africa House elicited the news that on leaving jail he had been promptly rearrested.

There followed a series of convoluted negotiations with South African diplomats. For several days Neville was almost a permanent fixture at South Africa House. An appeal to the Minister of Justice finally did the trick. Our man was given a clear choice by his gaolers: departure to East Grinstead within forty-eight hours or a prolonged stay behind bars. It was the most curious form of academic recruitment, but not out of line with Dr Simonsen's style of leadership.

Another intense round of diplomatic activity was set off by the director's private affairs. He met and fell in love with a French girl, who after six months of living-in showed distinct signs of pregnancy. Since no one liked to interfere in an entirely personal matter and since Dr Simonsen did not ask for advice, the couple were left to make their own maternity arrangements. Going for the best they booked in at University College Hospital where, I fancy, Dr Simonsen's robust views on childbirth (he did not believe in long confinements) and related gynaecological matters brought him into conflict with the authorities.

In any event, an over-attentive administrator, finding that an unmarried foreign national was about to give birth on the premises, reported the event to the Home Office. The poor girl was then denigrated as 'a burden on the taxpayer' and served with a deportation order. All hell broke out. In a brief but cogent meeting with Dr Simonsen, we were made to understand that if one had to go, both would go.

'I am not prepared to live in a country which expels pregnant girlfriends,' he declared, conjuring up images of shiploads of unmarried mothers setting off for distant shores.

'You could marry her,' I suggested, knowing full well what his answer would be.

'I am not prepared to be bullied into marriage by the British authorities.'

The prospect of losing a director in midstream, as it were, was too catastrophic to contemplate. It was a case of action now. Our only strong card was my Home Office contacts assiduously cultivated in my time with the refugee movement. I made full and unprincipled use of them with the result that the normal procedures were interrupted to allow for the reluctant issue of a resident's permit.

As I commented to John Watson,' 'I had no idea the academic world could be so stressful.'

In six years at East Grinstead, Morten Simonsen did not find all the answers. He did not expect to. But, as Neville prophesied, he certainly put us on the map. In the Simonsen period much was learned about ways of extending the life of grafted tissue and organs by chemical means and by close matching between individuals. He built up a vigorous and dedicated team of scientists who made the McIndoe Centre a leader in immunological research. Some measure of Dr Simonsen's achievement was his appointment by the Royal College of Surgeons as Honorary Professor in Transplantation Research.

The adaptation of pure research to the treatment of patients begged the need for more specialist facilities at the Queen Victoria. A much favoured idea, first mooted when Archie was still alive, was for a Burns Centre. But the sheer novelty of the idea (there was nowhere in the world where we could draw on experience) made for a hazy estimate of costs. All we knew for certain was that it would take a huge amount of money – far in excess of the sum spent on the research centre.

We were drawn towards a decision by John Watson's painstaking search for a workable scheme and by the knowledge that every time we re-examined the idea, the cost had edged up a few thousand. Unless we acted soon, we decided, the Burns Centre really would move beyond our reach.

With the Blond and Marks families working in unison, close on a quarter of a million pounds was raised. This took care of the building and equipment. The NHS was to cover the running costs, a highly satisfactory arrangement which gave further evidence that government and voluntary effort could coexist. But my faith in bureaucratic goodwill took a knock a few months later when, after the opening of the Burns Centre, the Queen Victoria was presented with a supplementary rates bill. I have no doubt the council treasurer was merely applying the law, but at the time it did seem a case of having the cake and eating it.

Compensatory news came from the Rayne Foundation, which decided to back the formation of a burns research team to work alongside the other scientists already investigating new techniques in transplantation.

Morten Simonsen was succeeded by John Batchelor from the Department of Immunology at Guys Hospital. Under his tutelage, research into the close matching of grafts to their recipients was given top priority. It was in Professor Batchelor's time that a great advance was made in prolonging the life of transplanted kidneys by the careful choice of a compatible donor.

The discovery of a way to keep skin alive almost indefinitely by storing it at low temperatures in liquid nitrogen led to the setting up of a skin bank. This eased the problem of finding suitable grafts for emergency operations. In one case donated skin survived for ninety-three days as against the usual fourteen to twenty-one days.

Greater expertise was gained in the joining of small blood vessels, which helped in the reattachment of severed fingers or toes. John Cobbett put up a surgical milestone when he transferred a patient's big toe to replace a lost thumb.

The finest compliment to the Blond-McIndoe Centre was the demand on its services by doctors throughout the world. By the late 1960s, the pressure on laboratory staff to advise on tissue typing cases became so great that the research programme was put at risk. The crisis was not resolved until the NHS was persuaded to take over this part of the work.

We all knew we were at the edge of a huge expansion in transplantation surgery. The work at East Grinstead and in other younger research centres dotted about the world was rapidly taking us towards the day when miracles of heart and lung transplants would make headline news.

But the challenge thrown out by Archie back in the war years, to find a sure way of controlling the body's immune system, had still to be met. There was a lot of work yet to do.

Great Days at the Royal Court

It was Edward Blacksell – Blackie of Guinea Pig fame – who introduced Neville to the English Stage Company, and it was Neville who introduced the English Stage Company to the Royal Court. Their ambition was laudable but modest: to create a showcase for new writers. I do not believe either of them ever dreamt of starting a cultural revolution. If they did, they neglected to tell me.

To take the story back to the beginning, Blackie's resumption of school-mastering in the West Country was the signal for a flurry of community activities for which he and his talented wife, Joan, were guiding spirits. One of their happiest inspirations was the Devon Festival, which they started with the writer Ronald Duncan. The Festival was a success but, for Ronnie, realization did not measure up to expectation. The programme had too much music and too little drama for his liking. To restore the balance, he and Blackie tried hard to persuade leading production companies to spend a few days in Devon. None would. So they set up their own production company – with a working capital of £50 out of their own pockets – and came up to London to lobby their theatrical contacts. Lord Harewood, who had also abetted the Devon Festival, was an early recruit to the cause. His suggestion for putting a name to their efforts – the English Stage Company – was inspired by his own, already established, English Opera Group.

Another useful ally was Oscar Lewenstein, one of the more imaginative of producers and a hero of the Devon Festival, for whom he had laid on Joan Littlewood's Theatre Workshop to play *Mother Courage*.

A council was formed and meetings held. The idea took hold that maybe they were limiting themselves unfairly by tying the English Stage Company too closely to the Devon Festival. If new writing was worth supporting, then why not where it really counted, in London. But dreams were free. They could not get close to reality until they had solid financial backing. At this point Blackie invited himself to dinner. I was openly amazed when Neville showed an interest. He

155

was not knowledgeable about the theatre, nor even very taken with the idea of it except as an undemanding night out.

Another thing: there was a view, which I must say I shared, that the live theatre had had its day. Everybody wanted to stay at home to watch television, and with the independent channel just opened the competition from that quarter was bound to intensify.

A sign of the times was the way in which the theatre and cinema had retreated into themselves, offering old and tried formulas in the hope of holding on to their core audiences. The West End theatre of the 1950s was much like the West End theatre of the 1930s, inspiring nothing more substantial than a sense of *déja vu* every time a young chap or gal entered through the French windows swinging a tennis racket.

'Precisely,' said Blackie. 'That's what's wrong with the West End. It's old-fashioned and tired. No wonder it can't stand up to television. We want try something different. We want to put on plays by younger writers for younger audiences.'

By 'younger' Blackie meant writers and audiences in their forties, which gives an idea of just how backward-looking the theatre had become.

Neville delivered the verdict of a businessman: 'You won't get far with a collection of people talking across a table. You need a base, somewhere people can identify with the English Stage Company. You need a theatre.'

'That's it,' shouted Blackie with huge delight. 'I knew you'd understand the problem. We need a theatre. And there's only one person who can get it for us.'

I did not believe him for a minute. Neither did Neville. But he gave a big laugh. He was hooked. I see now that he was looking for a challenge.

Buying a theatre was no problem; finding a theatre at the right price was difficult. The first realistic proposal came from Alfred Esdaile, who held the lease on the Kingsway Theatre. Esdaile was an unlikely associate of the English Stage Company. He was an impresario of some style who made a substantial living from the sort of risqué revues favoured by initiated males out for a night on the town. His great delight was in finding ways to skirt the rules of decency as defined by the Lord Chamberlain. The convention that nudes were allowed on stage only on condition that they did not move their bodies was circumvented by attaching the girls to wires and flying them over the audience. The performers did not move their bodies; Esdaile moved their bodies for them. It was a neat trick which gave the Lord Chamberlain a headache until the girls solved the problem on his behalf. They were prepared to reveal all, they told Esdaile, but not risk all. They demanded danger money. Esdaile did a quick calculation and ordered the nudes back on the stage. 'The worst that can happen to them there', he is reported as saying, 'is an attack of cramp.'

By 1955 it was a long time since the Kingsway had housed any sort of production. A casualty of the Blitz, the theatre had remained derelict for more than a decade. But it was going cheap – Esdaile was keen to be shot of it – and first estimates of the cost of renovation were not outrageous. Neville, who was impatient for action, silenced all reservations by a promise of cash on the table and a commitment to raise whatever else was needed. I was bowled over by his enthusiasm and mightily impressed by his skill in extracting money from narrow pockets, an exercise in which I considered myself an expert. His coup was to support Esdaile's election to the council of the English Stage Company and then to tap him for £1,000 towards the rebuilding of his own theatre.

While Neville concentrated on putting together the nuts and bolts, his colleagues looked about for someone to run the company. In those wilderness days, artistic directors with imagination and resolve were hard to come by. One name which came up early in discussions – and stayed the course – was George Devine, an actor turned director who had impressed with his work at the London Theatre Studio and at the Young Vic. The Arts Council approved of George (a vital factor if a grant was to be secured), but the only council member to have met him was Lewenstein. They had talked about plans which George had put together for a permanent company to present plays by neglected writers – plans which closely resembled those of the English Stage Company. At Oscar's insistence, a meeting was set up between George and Ronnie Duncan, who at this point was still the main arbiter of artistic policy. The two appeared to get on well; in any event, Ronnie endorsed George's appointment. It was not until the new artistic director was firmly installed that it became obvious that there was no agreement at all on what constituted good writing for the theatre.

George was the gutsy rebel who paraded his socialist credentials all the way to Aldermaston. He wanted a liberated – by which he meant radical – theatre. Ronnie too looked to escape from the dragnet of low-brow entertainment, but his interests went beyond the political and social to the higher plains of ethical reasoning and mysticism. His standards were set by Eliot and Fry with their verse dramas which he tried to emulate with his widely praised, if now forgotten, *This Way to the Tomb*. This contradiction of personalities had all the makings of a great and glorious row. We did not have to wait long for it to break out.

George started with the English Stage Company in March 1955. He brought with him as his associate a young former television producer, Tony Richardson. At this time, Neville was still persuaded that the Kingsway was a viable proposition. He was wrong. Every time he looked at the costs of reconstruction, the figure doubled. Then Esdaile came up with another idea. What about the Royal Court? Esdaile had bought a thirty-five year lease on the building in 1952. A tatty, run-down place (notwithstanding claims of extensive renovation), the box office had kept going on intimate reviews, latterly *Airs on a Shoestring*, staged by Laurie Lister. George, who knew the theatre and had even tried to get it for his own earlier project, was enthusiastic. Neville was swept along.

At a meeting a few weeks later, Neville startled the council members who were not yet in the know by announcing, 'I've bought the Royal Court. I hope you think it's a good idea.'

'We were speechless,' reported Blackie. 'I was sitting next to Peggy Ashcroft and even she went pale.'

The financial deal was a triumph for Neville. He bought the lease from Esdaile at a bargain price of £25,000 payable over ten years. Rent and rates accounted for another £6,000 a year. Cutting the immediate outgoings to the house meant there was some money in hand to pay for a few basic repairs like fixing the roof before it fell in and clearing the drains, which had the nasty habit of overflowing into the stalls.

Neville and I put £8,000 into the kitty, the Arts Council chipped in with about the same amount and Peter Jones, the store across the square from the Royal Court, made a handsome gift of £2,000. With guarantees from the wealthier ranks of the council, the budget began to look quite respectable.

Next came the little matter of finding a few plays. George had the notion of introducing well-known novelists to the stage, but there was no rush to take him up on his offer. A first play from Angus Wilson promised for the opening production was a transfer from the Bristol Old Vic and Ronnie was lined up with *Don Juan* and *The Peach of Satan*, both seen at the Devon Festival; otherwise there were no obvious candidates for the first season.

An ad in *The Stage* appealing for new plays brought in a clutch of well-thumbed manuscripts. Only one held George's interest. For £25 he bought the option on a play called *Look Back in Anger* by a young out-of-work actor called John Osborne.

It is part of the folklore of the theatre that Kenneth Tynan was alone in detecting the brilliance of *Look Back in Anger*. His ecstatic review in the *Observer* ('I doubt if I could love anyone who did not wish to see *Look Back in Anger*. It is the best young play of its decade') was worth waiting for, but the verdict of the overnight critics gave early encouragement. This was more than could be said of the ESC council, most of whom came down heavily against the play. The attack was led by Ronnie, who ridiculed George's idea of 'new drama'. 'What's new about it?' he demanded to know. As far as he could see the same old West End platitudes were being served up in a different guise: 'Instead of the Shaftesbury Avenue duchess fiddling with her flower vase we have Jimmy Porter picking his nose in public.' George fumed and plotted revenge.

Meanwhile, *Look Back in Anger* was still in need of an audience. Excited critics did not guarantee a queue at the box office. It was, in its time, a difficult play. The problem was not so much a matter of format – it was old-fashioned enough to have a neatly crafted beginning, middle and end – or of context, but of substance. What precisely was Osborne trying to get across? His anti-hero, Jimmy Porter, mounted a devastating assault on the inadequacies of post-war Britain, but had nothing to say on what was to be done. In failing to offer solutions, the play was without hope. How depressing!

159

But what rule was there that says in drama, or in any other art form, that problems could only be started when accompanied by answers? Osborne was to strike a chord with a lot of educated young people who felt hemmed in by the old guard. They too were unsure as to what they wanted, but they knew frustration.

Sensing this, George Fearon, who did publicity for the Royal Court, suggested putting an extract of the play on television. It was, he said, 'The best way of getting the message across to Osborne's generation'. On this, as on so many others issues, the council dithered. George Fearon had to overcome the fears of those who believed that any further exposure of the play would kill it dead. But he prevailed and proved his point by filling the house.

By the time the play returned to the Royal Court for an extended run, George Fearon had invented and exploited the Angry Young Man, a tag which Osborne was to share with Kingsley Amis, John Wain, Colin Wilson and others adopted by the new generation as their own. Thereafter *Look Back in Anger* was assured of capacity business.

The English Stage Company needed a success. The earlier two productions, Angus Wilson's *The Mulberry Bush* and a transfer from Broadway of Arthur Miller's *The Crucible*, failed to generate more than mild critical disdain. But the real disaster of the season was fourth in line. Two full-length plays by Ronnie were cut to make a double-bill. Why he agreed to it I have no idea. He was convinced that George Devine, as director, was out to destroy his work. He could well have been right since it is hard to imagine how an event as mind-numbing as *The Death of Satan* could have been presented with any other thought in mind. After eight performances to near empty houses, the plays were withdrawn.

While George and Ronnie intensified their vendetta over what constituted good drama, Neville concentrated on the figures. By his reckoning, John Osborne was the only new writer (and the Royal Court was committed to new writing) who could balance the books. There were two ways in which Neville could help to achieve this – by negotiating a transfer of *Look Back in Anger* to the West End and by encouraging Osborne to finish his next play.

The first required tactful handling of the Arts Council, who took the puritanical view that public subsidy should not be used, even indirectly, to help mount a purely commercial production. There were those at the Royal Court who warned him of a likely Arts Council boycott, but he was adamant. He told his critics: 'In business we invest in success; theatre is entertainment business, therefore we must exploit our success.'

He carried the argument with the Arts Council, though not without much tut-tutting along the way. After a return to the Royal Court in October, *Look Back in Anger* went to the West End and from thence to Broadway, where the New York Critics Circle voted it best foreign play of the season.

But until the royalty cheques started arriving, Osborne remained the struggling playwright who had to find some way of making a living. Neville bought the option on his next three plays and arranged for him to receive a £9 a week salary while he finished *The Entertainer*.

Everybody expected another attack on the system and to that extent they were not disappointed. *The Entertainer*, as Tynan was later to observe, 'put the whole of contemporary England on to one and the same stage. It is John Osborne's diagnosis of the sickness that is currently afflicting our slap-happy land.' But the Royal Court's artistic committee, consisting of George Harewood, Ronnie Duncan and Oscar Lewenstein, were less than enthusiastic. George was the only one to declare unreserved support. The other two thought the play was a mess. How could you make serious drama out of a tatty old music-hall routine? Even when they heard that Laurence Olivier, no less, was interested in playing the lead, they were not convinced.

Hoping to avoid another open conflict between Ronnie and George Devine, Neville responded to an appeal from George Harewood to arrange a round-table meeting. The artistic committee were invited to lunch at Orchard Court.

My husband chose to be diplomatic. Suspecting that Ronnie would dig his heels in if he thought he was up against a heavy weight, Neville steered away from any suggestion that personal pride was at stake. Instead, he took the line that the Royal Court had a responsibility to Osborne: he was their writer, an undoubtedly talented young man, who deserved their support. 'We owe it to the boy,' declared Neville.

The discussion meandered around this theme until I could stand it no longer. I banged the table: 'It'll make money. Isn't that what you want? With Olivier in the play you'd have to be barmy to turn it down.' Everyone went quiet after that. I felt they had taken the point.

The Entertainer was a success – for Osborne, for Olivier, for Tony Richardson who directed and, not least, for the Royal Court. After a four-week sell-out the play went on to the Palace Theatre and to Broadway, creating in its wake a tidy revenue which did much to sustain the English Stage Company. In five years, Osborne's plays brought in over £60,000, twice the Arts Council grant for the same period.

Osborne's triumph strengthened George Devine's claim to put on what he wanted instead of what the artistic committee, led by Ronnie, thought best for him. Given the choice, Neville had greater sympathy for George, who seemed to him to be more at home on the assault course that was contemporary drama. For this reason he rejected Ronnie's hysterical protest when George assumed the right to overrule the artistic committee.

But this did not mean he favoured total freedom for the creative spirit. That way was financial disaster. With the theatre's overdraft (which Neville guaranteed) climbing alarmingly, there was an urgent need to balance minority drama with shows of wider and more profitable appeal. George refused to recognize the distinction, partly out of loyalty to his writers and directors – I never knew him to say a bad word about any of them. At the same time, there was a dangerous leaning towards the assumption of infallibility. With every disaster, and there were quite a few, the blame was put on unsympathetic critics or unsophisticated audiences, never on those who were responsible for the productions.

The verdict today might go to George for his backing of John Arden, Eugène Ionesco and a few other writers unappreciated in their time, but distance has done nothing to add to the dramatic reputation of Nigel Dennis and Angus Wilson or to raise the appeal of plays like Ann Jellicoe's *The Sport of My Mad Mother*. I have spent some weary evenings in the Royal Court.

This is not to suggest that George was anything but a brilliant man of the theatre. His niche in history is secured, if for no other reason than his talent-spotting of John Osborne, N. F. Simpson and the brilliant Arnold Wesker, then the only portraitist of working-class people who did not patronize them. But George could be, and often was, wrong.

To introduce what Neville called 'sympathetic restraint', he brought in as business manager Robin Fox, the charming if wayward husband of our long-standing friend Angela Fox and father of what was to be the theatrical triumvirate of Edward, James and Robert. Trained as a lawyer, Robin had worked in the London office of the Music Corporation of America, then the world's biggest show-business agency. Robin was soon indispensable to the running of the Royal Court, the in-between man who alone understood both the language of business and of the arts, and was prepared to interpret impartially.

But even Robin could not hold the ring between George and Ronnie. Their fight went into the final round in 1960, when Ronnie put together a catalogue of complaints against 'the socialist clique', who, he said, dominated the Royal Court. I wondered at his naivety in seeing George as the director liked to see himself, as a class rebel who was set to overthrow the established order. In fact, George's radicalism never went so far as to disturb a comfortable and, in many ways, a conventional life. He and his Oxbridge colleagues were unashamedly elitist and were not averse to feathering each other's nests – just like old-fashioned capitalists. I treasure a comment by Lindsay Anderson: '. . . by chance, George Devine, Tony Richardson and I were all ex-Wadham men!' By chance, my foot.

There were one or two on the council who took Ronnie's red-scare tactics seriously, but they quickly backed off when he made the mistake of leaking his accusations to the press. The English Stage Company closed ranks and gave George a unanimous vote of confidence.

Little more was heard of Ronnie. He remained on the council, swingeing from the sidelines but seldom finding a target. Maybe he felt he no longer had to try very hard. George was clearly not in the best of health. He tired very easily and was absent from the theatre for long periods. A disastrous attempt to do for Rex Harrison what the Court had done for Olivier (in a Nigel Dennis play, *August for the People*) led to George having a nervous breakdown. In 1965 he announced his retirement, choosing the occasion, a critic's lunch at the Savoy, to pay generous tribute to Neville. A few weeks later, George had the first of a series of heart attacks. Within a year he was dead and Ronnie, pausing only to avoid the memorial service, had resigned from the council.

Around the mid-1960s, the English Stage Company showed distinct signs of falling apart. It did not help that the Royal Court was closed for almost a year, though it certainly needed its renovation. Whenever we went to a first night, a line from *The Entertainer* inevitably came to mind: 'Don't clap too loud, lady; it's an old building.'

But at the heart of the crisis was the loss of purpose and sense of direction. Now that the Royal Shakespeare Company was chasing London audiences and the National was settled in at the Old Vic, the English Stage Company could no longer command the loyalty of the avant-garde. Even in the context of new writing, there was strong competition from Joan Littlewood's Theatre Royal at Stratford East where productions like *Fings Ain't Wot They Used T'Be, Oh! What A Lovely War* and *Mrs Wilson's Diary* stole the limelight – and the critics' hearts.

Meanwhile, much of the creative energy of the English Stage Company had passed to Woodfall Films, named after a street off the King's Road, where John Osborne, Tony Richardson and others were busy with the latest revival of the British film industry.

The box office had a disastrous year in 1965. Thereafter some semblance of financial order was restored by the reinstatement of short runs and a mixed programme of new and familiar plays. But the shadow of the Arts Council creditors still hovered, and relations between the council and professionals remained uncomfortably tense.

My chief concern was for Neville. That he took pleasure from the Royal Court (even the in-fighting had its moments of exultation) I had no doubt, but the strain of a frenetic life was beginning to tell.

In 1966 he was seventy, but looked older. He might have stayed healthier if he had stuck to his prescribed diet, but he loved his food and was not prepared, as he put it, 'to live like a hermit just for a few extra years'.

He had wonderful doctors, but what kept him going was the dominance of will over disability. In his last year, ignoring all advice, he insisted on coming with me to Israel. It was a fraught journey with me worrying all the time and Neville telling me to stop nagging, which must have made everybody think I had turned into a dreadful harridan. It was not as if he was a devoted Zionist, but together we did the full social round, including the Jerusalem Baby House and the Blond Crèche in Tel Aviv. Neville said all the right things to our hosts while telling me – which I thought was a bit rich – that more ought to be done in Israel to provide decent social services.

In the pile of correspondence awaiting our return there was one letter which gave Neville enormous pleasure. He was to be made a Fellow of the Royal College of Surgeons. It was an honour I was to share a few years later, so I can vouch for the awesome experience of being inducted into that body of grandees. As your sponsor declaims your qualifications, you half expect him to throw in a few medical details. Would they not be of more interest to this dedicated company?

Shortly afterwards, Neville went into Guys Hospital. To his bedside came a succession of friends with whom he joked about his frailties. There was never a trace of self-pity. When Sol Cohen asked sympathetically about the food, Neville told him, 'At least, melon is permissible.' And then, laughing, added, 'Port fed, of course.'

Towards the end, when we all knew that there was nothing to do except wait, Neville lost patience with the medical charade. Being covered with tubes, unable to do anything for himself, was not his idea of dignity. He wanted to call a stop, and he did.

The tributes to Neville were fulsome and generous, especially from the Royal Court. Arnold Wesker spoke of his 'great, wise tolerance', Joan Plowright remembered his sensitivity and understanding which sustained George Devine 'through many a black depression.' 'Without him', Oscar Lewenstein said, 'we might never have started.' The same thought recurred in letters from past and present champions of the McIndoe Centre, while dear friends like Sam Lieberman, a former Canadian fighter pilot and now a judge in Alberta, invoked the love of 'a multitude of friends'.

One of the loveliest letters was from the little daughter of the surgeon, Robin Beare:

> Dear Antie Alaine
> I am so sorry that Darling Uncle Nev died, but I am sure that he will go up to HAVEN.
> Lots of Love
> Virginia

It made me cry, but it also made me feel much better.

I must quote from one other letter. It is from Edward Fox, written in response to one of those frequent newspaper wrangles about precisely who did what to create the magic of the Royal Court:

My friendship with Neville began when I was, I suppose, eight or nine years old. Through early youth I worked in productions at the Court as a very junior and very ill-equipped actor: taking part in Osborne's *A Patriot for Me*, George Devine's own last performance at that theatre; also in several previous productions. I was greatly influenced by the life and atmosphere of that Theatre in early acting days. What young actor in this country could fail not to have been so. During all those years, I met and received the delights of Neville's greatly generous friendship very often.

If it can be assumed that the life of any successful theatrical enterprise depends, not on the contribution of one man's influence and energies, but on those of several, or many, then I take this to have been particularly true of the time that Neville was Chairman of the Royal Court Theatre. Theatrical life depends on a collective commitment.

During those years, the Royal Court achieved more truly innovatory success as a theatre of international fame and renown, producing writer's work that would not have been undertaken by any other London theatre at the time, and thereby creating a style of production and consistency of excellence that became a hallmark and was in itself a revolution of sorts in theatre terms. This all happened under the chairmanship of Neville Blond.

Chairmen of theatrical enterprises, because they are not actors, producers, writers and designers, do a type of work that seldom comes to public attention, because it is not essentially a type of work that interests the public, generally speaking, there being so many others in this line of country that are of public interest. None the less I do feel strongly that it should be publicly recognized that without the work that the Chairman and his Associates perform for the theatrical good, that can be witnessed by an onlooker nightly, the rich harvest that I have written of above could neither have been sown nor reaped. This is especially true of the Court Theatre which was always in difficulty to keep a continuous flow of new work in production from financial as well as every other aspect.

It is work that by its very nature is behind the scenes; continuous; hazardous; usually unthanked; requiring immense stamina and belief in an ideal; and as much courage and commitment as does any other part of a theatrical venture.

People of the theatre are infinitely lucky in that they choose their profession, and they give to it their heart's love willingly. I always feel we are like people who are fortunately offered a lease for life and a beautiful property, which is ours for life to invest in and make of what we will, and after our lease ends, we leave a legacy. The beauty of the property and the legacy left behind by Neville Blond's chairmanship of the Royal Court Theatre speaks for itself, and is something that our English Theatre can be and should be unqualifiably and justly proud of, and Neville Blond's name on that Roll of Honour should need no explanation for the love and duty that he bequeathed as our legacy.

I have no doubt that when Edward wrote his letter he was thinking also of his father, Robin, who died, tragically early, just six months after Neville. For that brief period he was joint chairman of the English Stage Company with Oscar Lewenstein. But his steady good sense was at its premium when, working with Neville, he had to take the brunt of the conflict with the Arts Council and the Critics Circle over Lindsay Anderson's calculated snub of the *Spectator*. Its reviewer, Hilary Spurling, was refused first-night tickets because the director did not find her 'attitude to our work illuminating'. Immediately almost everybody went over the top. There were wild accusations of sabotage by the company who had suffered Miss Spurling's jagged barbs, and of censorship by the critics. The council, as ever, was divided in its opinion. Neville was no longer up to the task of reconciliation, but Robin managed it.

With both of them gone, the Royal Court was short on resilience and self-assurance.

A New Generation

Like many others in my position, I smothered grief by hard work. The FWZ kept me busy and, while I was conscious of the risks of seeming to tread in Neville's footsteps, I felt close enough to the affairs of the McIndoe Centre (soon to be known as the Blond-McIndoe Centre) to take over there as chairman and to the Royal Court to accept an invitation to become vice-chairman. One of the thrills at the Royal Court was overseeing the awards from the Neville Blond Fund set up in 1972 to encourage new writing.

But though the Royal Court was a prize not easily surrendered (I made no secret of enjoying the razzamatazz of the theatre), I soon wearied of the constant backbiting. The gulf between artistic purity and administrative practicality was always with us, but there was now another, nastier conflict to contend with.

It seemed to many of us that the political content of our productions was sliding so far to the left as to be frequently outside the democratic frame. To take the most obvious example, the work of Edward Bond, with its dependence on crude shock tactics, could not be separated from the author's declared view that violence was justified in changing what he regarded as an unjust society. Since most of us on the council qualified, for Bond, as perpetrators of the unjust society, it was not altogether clear why we should be expected to fight for money to allow him to promote our destruction. It was all the more galling that, on the evidence of seats occupied in the mercifully short runs of his plays, Bond was a minority interest.

So, indeed, were many of the other writers who were given the freedom of the Royal Court stage. Meanwhile, the deficit grew ever larger and the struggle to bring reality to the artistic proceedings ever tougher.

In 1976 the Arts Council, with total justification, told the Royal Court to pull its socks up or else. Before the grant was renewed the theatre 'had to evolve a programme which is at once artistically exciting and financially successful'.

Greville Poke, the former owner of *Everybody's*, who had been with the Royal Court from the beginning and was now chairman, accepted the challenge. At this point, Robert Kidd, one of the joint artistic directors, accused us of defiling the unique reputation of the Royal Court. Before storming out, he called for my resignation as president, the job in which I had recently succeeded George Harewood. It was all a little embarrassing since Robert was married to Jenny Sieff, daughter of Teddy and Lois Sieff. Lois, who certainly knew the theatre, was also involved in the Royal Court. It was no secret that Robert staked his future on winning her the presidency; he had actually canvassed in her support. But his involvement was counter-productive to his aims. With the warning signals flashing from the Arts Council, few council members were keen to strengthen the position of Robert and his co-artistic director, Nicholas Wright. So even those who were sympathetic to Lois pushed their votes my way.

With Robert's departure, we could say openly what we had been saying in private for several weeks, that we wanted a more mature personality to run the theatre, someone with artistic flair who, to quote a *Times* leader on the subject, 'was not afraid of vulgar success'. A name which came up in conversation representing the ideal was that of Stuart Burge, an actor turned director who, in the late 1960s, had proved his worth as a rescuer of down-and-out theatres by reanimating the Nottingham Playhouse. A first meeting went well. The Royal Court evidently retained its pulling power. But there was an obstacle: Stuart had already been offered, and had accepted, a job at the National, where Peter Hall wanted him to run the Cottesloe Theatre.

It was touch and go for a while, and I have no doubt that Peter Hall did his best to freeze us out. But, as a pinnacle to his career, the Royal Court must have looked the better prospect to Stuart who, in the end, came our way. We all had reason to be grateful. Under his leadership the Royal Court started on the long haul back to solvency.

Today, the Royal Court is once again the home of exciting new drama, one of the few British theatres to hold out a welcome to young writers, actors and directors. I do not agree with everything they do, but I cannot say I am ever bored. Perhaps I am more tolerant – though Edward Bond is still beyond the pale. Soon after the Brighton bomb went off at the Conservative Party Conference, he wrote a poem praising the terrorists. It was printed in a Royal Court programme for one of his plays. As I read it, my distaste for Mr Bond and all his works was sharpened by the knowledge that among those caught in the blast was my daughter, Simone.

At the Blond-McIndoe Centre, pioneering work of a different kind was making spectacular progress. The central purpose, of achieving complete control over the body's immune system, remained, and still remains, an elusive target, but the steady accumulation of knowledge about the way individual molecules operate within the body was opening up exciting chances for manipulating the immune system in certain ways.

The use of vaccines to combat diseases like polio and smallpox had shown what could be done. Now there was a real possibility of identifying the cells which turn against the body in such disabling diseases as rheumatoid arthritis and multiple sclerosis. This, in turn, held out the prospect of spotting potential victims at a stage where preventative treatment could be effective.

Another breakthrough was the discovery of purified human growth factor in the membrane surrounding babies in the womb. It was found that laying a piece of the membrane on a wound before a skin graft improved the chances of its success. This was because the membrane stimulated the growth of blood cells. In this way the skin graft was given the nourishment to survive.

But the greatest advance was in creating laboratory conditions in which living cultured skin could actually grow. The treatment of major burns advanced substantially as a result.

From the view of those who were holding up the financial props it was unnerving how the main flow of research created a need for supplementary projects. As John Watson observed: 'The more you find out, the more you realize how complex the problems are.' And expensive, he might have added. By the late 1970s, the Centre needed over a quarter of a million a year just to keep going.

Always on the look-out for money-raising ideas, I found that, with the advance in age, my birthday celebrations were a great stimulus to fund-raising. To mark my seventy-fifth year friends clubbed together to set up an Elaine Blond scholarship in microvascular research. I think that might reasonably qualify as a present for the woman who has everything.

I wish I could say I understand the science in even broadest detail. Alas, it is not so and never likely to be. I am constantly amazed how knowledgeable Peter and Simone are who, as the latest front-runners among the trustees, keep me up to date.

Still, I must not get obsessed by research. The Plastic Surgery Department, the McIndoe Burns Unit and the Corneo-Plastic Unit at the Queen Victoria Hospital are among the best in the world.

Not long ago I mentioned this to a friend who then told me he had recently spent an hour at the hospital having a prominent cyst removed from the bridge of his nose. Though a simple operation, he was given the full treatment. Wheeled into the theatre to meet a panoply of medical talent, he just had time to say hello before a light bandage was placed over his eyes and he was absorbing the local anaesthetic. Next, there was the most terrible crash as, he found out later, a nurse tripped with a dish of instruments. There was a short pause before the sister bent towards the patient and whispered in his ear: 'No need to worry. That was the surgeon fainting at the sight of blood.'

I loved this story because it proved, if proof was needed, that the spirit of Archie McIndoe lived on.

Marks and Spencer without Simon was unthinkable – until the unthinkable happened. On 8 December 1964, in the middle of a row with a departmental head, he had a heart attack and dropped dead.

In his memoirs Israel Sieff makes a revealing comment on Simon. 'Since he died,' he wrote, 'I have in one sense felt a freer person; my decisions and judgements are not related to those of anybody else as they were to Simon's.' I know what he means. Throughout my life I deferred to Simon even to the point of not wearing earrings in his presence. For some reason he had an intense dislike of those items of jewellery.

He was dominating, self-opinionated and single-minded in his determination to get his own way. He was also clever, far-seeing and passionately loyal to colleagues who did their jobs. It was easy to hate him, but not for long. His eccentricities (his aversion to earrings was one of many) endeared him even to those who feared his sharp tongue.

For Simon, life was work. He could not bear to waste a minute. It was, I think, more for this reason than for any affectation that he

171

was always accompanied by an entourage of colleagues, secretaries and assistants. Even in the corridors of Michael House, he could be heard firing off instructions or throwing out ideas at the confidants who followed at his heels. David Susman recalls a meeting which started in Simon's office, continued into the corridor as Simon set off to some unannounced destination, and concluded in the men's lavatory where conversation proceeded more or less unimpeded through the closed door of one of the cubicles.

There was a dour side to Simon's personality, revealed most palpably in his dislike of all restaurants (which he assumed to be unhygenic) and his preference for Spartan meals delivered on a tray. It was said that this was the reason why he never had an affair. Women were attracted to him and he to them, but there was no crossing the culinary divide.

He could be companionable and entertaining, but his best jokes were at the expense of others. A story which went the full round of the family was of his interview with the buyer responsible for a sub-standard batch of men's pyjamas. A higher quality sample was brought to Simon's office for inspection.

'Well, put them on, put them on,' commanded Simon of the buyer. 'I can't be expected to judge properly with you just holding them up.'

Sheepishly, the man did as he was told. Simon walked twice round the reluctant model. 'Good. Excellent. They'll do nicely.'

Enormously relieved, the buyer started changing back into business attire. Simon stopped him: 'You can't do that here – What do you think this is, a changing-room?'

A minute later, startled passers-by were treated to the sight of a pyjama-clad senior manager, clutching his pinstripe suit, sliding down the corridor towards the refuge of his own office.

The two dominant personalities of the Marks family died within a year of each other. Unlike Simon, Becky ended her days without that happy sense of a job well done. She had achieved much, but her failure to gain recognition outside her own close group of admirers made her resentful and bitter. In part, her problem was one of success breeding success. Israel was a young, fast-growing country in which the founding generation was quickly pushed aside by newcomers eager to control events.

But Becky never quite lost her spirit of adventure or her sense of the outrageous. Driving through Tel Aviv to a WIZO meeting, she upbraided her chauffeur for his apparent lack of urgency.

'Why do you keep stopping?' she demanded to know.

'But, Madam, it is the traffic lights. I have to stop when they are at red.'

The excuse was unacceptable. 'Drive on,' commanded Becky, 'I was here long before the traffic lights.'

She was buried at Tel Mond not far from the house she and Israel had built twenty-five years earlier. Three thousand mourners came to her funeral. Among them were many Arabs, saddened, like us all, by the loss of a steadfast friend. Becky was born before her time. Today she would be a political or business leader of much greater eminence, but she showed the way. Those who followed could be grateful for the example and for the best piece of advice ever handed out to the feminist movement: 'Take your work seriously, ladies. But never take yourselves seriously.'

To his successors, Simon bequeathed an enterprise which was in peak condition. Having created the biggest retailer in the country he spent the last years of his life making sure it would stay at the top. The campaign known as Good Housekeeping cut out waste and sharpened efficiency. War was declared on the time-wasters. In the reception area to Michael House stood a miniature Nelson's Column with a register next to it showing how many forms and other routine documents had been cut the preceding month. In less than half a year, the accumulated saving of paper was higher than Nelson's Column. Simon judged any form which he could not understand as unnecessary. With some chairmen this might have invited a cynical riposte, but no one dared suggest that Simon was incapable of taking on any job in the company.

At the height of the Good Housekeeping Campaign, an extension to the head office in Baker Street was opened. It was designed to accommodate a staff of 2,000; it was no surprise when only 1,500 moved in.

The year 1964 was one of boardroom musical chairs. After thirty-eight years as vice-chairman and joint managing director, Israel Sieff took over the leadership with Teddy Sieff as his deputy. As the elder statesman, Israel was not expected to stay in the job for very long. But while it was assumed that Teddy would replace him (he did so in 1967 when Israel became president), he too was cast by age as a likely stop-gap before the younger generation came to power.

Of that group, there was no doubt as to who was the most ambitious. Marcus was like his father Israel in every respect except his willingness to remain long as a second-in-command. As personnel director he had implemented Simon's strategy for Good Housekeeping with a determination which offended the sensibilities of some of his more staid colleagues. One of the casualties was Flora Solomon who, as arbiter of staff welfare, had come to think of herself as immune from unpalatable commercial considerations. Now, as joint vice-chairman, Marcus was building up the food department to be the most profitable in the company.

His closest rival for the succession was Michael Sacher, the elder son of Harry and Miriam. He too was much like his father, sharing a fine intellect but with the defect of seeming to fight shy from the extrovert world of business. Michael was the arch-administrator, but Marcus was the man who made things happen.

Still, Marcus never made the mistake of assuming he was invincible. I judge this from the ease with which I could tease him into self-assertion. At one of the many lively dinners at Gotwick, I asked him who he thought would come after Teddy. He grunted a non-committal reply.

'Of course, Michael *is* senior to you.'

Marcus exploded. 'He most certainly is *not* senior to me.'

'Not in title, perhaps, but he is senior in age.'

Marcus puffed on a large cigar. 'Age', he declared grandly, 'has nothing to do with it.'

Possibly not, but it did take several years to fight off the challenge from Michael. Whatever the difference in talents, the Sacher interest was backed by a substantial shareholding which could not be ignored. It was not until 1970, when Marcus was appointed sole vice-chairman, that he could assume himself to be safely in the lead. Two years later, shortly after the death of his father, Marcus – or as he now was, Sir Marcus – moved into the chairman's office. Marks and Spencer prepared for another change of style.

The quality I admired most in Marcus was his willingness to come out from behind the office door. Though enormously influential outside the closed world of Marks and Spencer, Simon was not a great public figure; Teddy likewise chose to keep a low profile. But Marcus was not averse to giving his opinion on national issues that were relevant to his knowledge and experience. Thus, managers and trade unionists who talked and acted as if they were still in the industrial dark age came in for his waspish disapproval. Against them he preached the gospel of St Michael ('If it's not good enough for the boss, it's not good enough for anyone'), leading the *Observer* to suggest that if the nation wanted a government of all the talents, it would be tempting simply to hand over the job to Marks and Spencer.

Sensitive to the need for keeping the family atmosphere alive within the company, Marcus made good use of his aged aunt. As the last daughter of Michael Marks, I was a star turn at board luncheons, long service presentations and at pensioners' parties. It was not quite the involvement I had half hoped for in earlier years, but it was great fun.

Or mostly it was great fun. The risks of showing off in newspaper interviews or at public functions were brought home to me when there was a near successful attempt to murder Teddy Sieff. We were warned regularly by Scotland Yard of likely atrocities by Black September, the Palestine Liberation Front and other anti-Zionist groups. But terrorism seemed a world away until an unknown assassin shot Teddy in his own home.

It was a miracle that he lived. At the Middlesex Hospital where he had an emergency operation to remove the bullet, doctors concluded his life had been saved by good teeth. Healthy canines slowed down the momentum of the bullet to stop it severing vital blood vessels to the brain. But if the aim had been a fraction higher or lower, Teddy would not have had a chance.

In any event, no further risks were to be taken. Bomb-resistant and bullet-proof glass was ordered for the Baker Street headquarters, police guards were provided for sensitive meetings, and all of us had to have our mail screened before it was opened.

Teddy showed some style by going off on holiday as soon as they let him out of hospital. For good measure, three months later, he accepted the presidency of the Zionist Federation.

A Sort of Retirement

So here it is. Eighty. Who would have thought it. A few days ago I tried one of those health tests much favoured by the Sunday supplements. You give yourself plus or minus points on such questions as 'Do you take regular exercise?' or 'When did you last see a doctor?' to find out how long you are likely to survive. By my reckoning I should have been dead at seventy. So there is something else to be thankful for.

I have had a splendid party organized by Simone and Ann. Five hundred of my dearest who packed the Goldsmiths' Hall drank St. Michael's champagne and were serenaded by the English Chamber Orchestra. And I did not even have to make a speech. WIZO put on a 'This Is Your Life' in which David Frost escorted me back over the years – all happy memories. And I am the proud recipient of an OBE 'for charity and public service work'.

There is, I understand, more to come. After an induction into the Royal College of Surgeons, where I will be the lone woman out of thirty-four honorary Fellows, I am off again to Israel. There, as joint president of Britain's FWZ, I will be chairing a session of our first conference in the country for which we have all worked so hard.

I am very fortunate. I have friends and family around me. I see a lot, but never quite enough, of my grandchildren. My brain works overtime trying to keep pace with the diverse talents of my fondest companions – Stanley Baron, Stephen Mitchell, Chaim Raphael; from Blond-McIndoe, the Watsons, the Beares and the Bennets and, when the Canadians are in town, Bud Sugarman, Sam Lieberman and Sol Kannee.

I take pleasure in travelling, visiting and going out to the theatre. My collection of pictures, built up over twenty years and encompassing a fair range of my favourite Impressionists, is a continuing delight to me, if a headache to my insurance broker.

I spend the week in London at Orchard Court, a stone's throw from the Oxford Street Marks and Spencer where I do most of my shopping. At the weekend, I am in the country at Gotwick. I would not call it peaceful, exactly. There are too many visitors and too many obstreperous bridge players for the house to qualify as a retreat. But that is the way I like it.

I am at an age when young people ask: what is the secret? And I say: there is no secret. You just go on.

Afterword

Elaine Blond died on 11 November 1985. Her death was quick and painless. She phoned Ann one morning to say that she had a headache and had cancelled her attendance at the annual JIA dinner. She added that she would be round the next day to see her great-grandson. That evening the doctor called for a routine check-up. She died as she was talking to him. An hour later, the top table at the JIA dinner was almost empty as her family left to pay her their last respects and to comfort each other.

Elaine had decided to write her memoirs some twelve months before her death and had already started putting them on tape with the help of Barry Turner. We felt that it would be right to complete the book, and Barry Turner has managed to do this by meticulously filling in the missing details. We owe him an enormous debt of gratitude.

Elaine's special projects have been carried on as her living memory. The Blond-McIndoe Centre is still pursuing the sort of research that was always so close to her heart – skin transplantation. The Centre marked its twenty-fifth anniversary in 1987. Simone has taken over the reins there. The Burns Unit is still being used at the Queen Victoria Hospital.

Her generous legacy to WIZO enabled them to build a wonderful new playground in her name at her beloved Jerusalem Baby Home. The Israel Museum in Jerusalem received her favourite Impressionist painting by Pissarro. And the records of all the early work at the Central British Fund have been taped for posterity, including the minutes of all the meetings of the RCM from the early 1930s, so that researchers can use this archive in the future.

Elaine's death was the end of an era, her way of life never to be repeated. Her standards were high and she expected her family to maintain them. She was in her way a great matriarch – and we all loved her very much.

Ann Susman and Simone Prendergast
1988

FAMILY TREE

FAMILY TREE

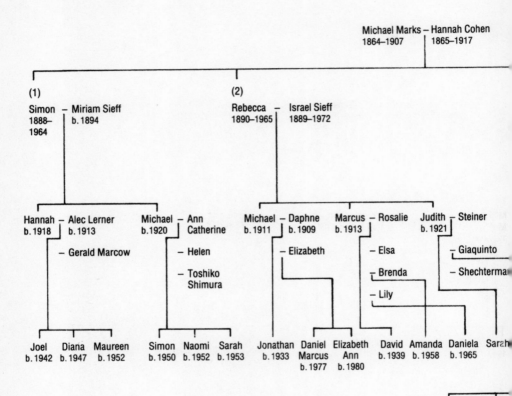

Michael Marks – Hannah Cohen
1864–1907 | 1865–1917

(1)
Simon – Miriam Sieff
1888– | b. 1894
1964

(2)
Rebecca – Israel Sieff
1890–1965 | 1889–1972

Hannah – Alec Lerner
b. 1918 | b. 1913

– Gerald Marcow

Michael – Ann
b. 1920 | Catherine

– Helen

– Toshiko
Shimura

Michael – Daphne
b. 1911 | b. 1909

– Elizabeth

Marcus – Rosalie
b. 1913

– Elsa

– Brenda

– Lily

Judith – Steiner
b. 1921

– Giaquinto

– Shechterma

Joel
b. 1942

Diana
b. 1947

Maureen
b. 1952

Simon
b. 1950

Naomi
b. 1952

Sarah
b. 1953

Jonathan
b. 1933

Daniel
Marcus
b. 1977

Elizabeth
Ann
b. 1980

David
b. 1939

Amanda
b. 1958

Daniela
b. 1965

Sarah

Marcus
Daniel

Michaela

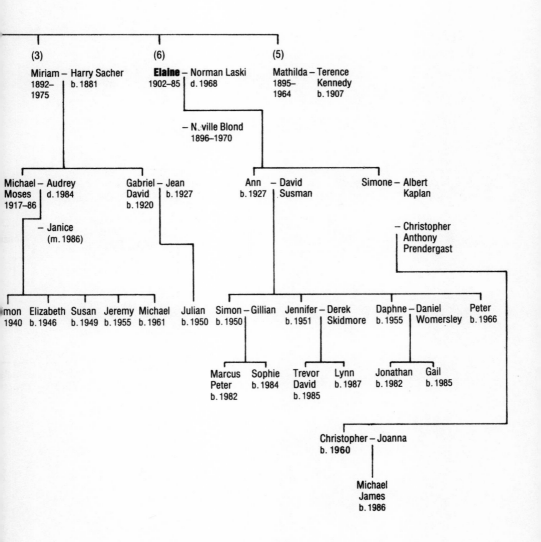

(3)
Miriam – Harry Sacher
1892– | b. 1881
1975

(6)
Elaine – Norman Laski
1902–85 | d. 1968

(5)
Mathilda – Terence
1895– | Kennedy
1964 | b. 1907

– N.ville Blond
1896–1970

Michael – Audrey
Moses | d. 1984
1917–86
| – Janice
| (m. 1986)

Gabriel – Jean
David | b. 1927
b. 1920

Ann – David
b. 1927 | Susman

Simone – Albert
| Kaplan

– Christopher
Anthony
Prendergast

imon Elizabeth Susan Jeremy Michael
1940 b. 1946 b. 1949 b. 1955 b. 1961

Julian
b. 1950

Simon – Gillian
b. 1950

Jennifer – Derek
b. 1951 | Skidmore

Daphne – Daniel
b. 1955 | Womersley

Peter
b. 1966

Marcus Sophie
Peter   b. 1984
b. 1982

Trevor Lynn
David   b. 1987
b. 1985

Jonathan Gail
b. 1982   b. 1985

Christopher – Joanna
b. 1960

Michael
James
b. 1986

INDEX

INDEX

INDEX